Kazunari Sakamoto. Lecture
坂本一成・講演

坂本一成・講演

編 ベアロッハー太央、サミュエル・スカッサビア

Quart 出版社

Kazunari Sakamoto. Lecture

Edited by Tao Baerlocher and Samuele Squassabia

Quart Publishers

まえがき 6
ベアロッハー太央、サミュエル・スカッサビア

自由な空間を求めて 10
序論

閉じた箱 16
散田の家 / 水無瀬の町家 / 雲野流山の家

家型 32
代田の町家 / 南湖の家 / 坂田山附の家 / 今宿の家 / 散田の共同住宅 / 祖師谷の家

自由な架構と広がりの領域 64
Project KO / Project S / House F

都市への開放 76
コモンシティ星田 / 熊本市営託麻団地 / 幕張ベイタウン・パティオス4番街

建築の解放 94
House SA / Hut T / QUICO 神宮前

スモール・コンパクト・ユニットとアイランド・プラン 116
Egota House / 工作連盟ジードルング・ヴィーゼンフェルト / Munich 2018 Winter Olympic Village

現実条件との葛藤による構成形式 134
東工大蔵前会館 / 宇土市立網津小学校

閉じた箱の開放 150
水無瀬の別棟 / 改築 散田の家

オーディナリーな解放的空間 162
結論

建築を考える自由 170
長谷川豪

付録 176
略歴 / 著作 / 作品目録

7 Foreword
Tao Baerlocher, Samuele Squassabia

11 The search for the free space
Introduction

17 The closed box
House in Sanda / Townhouse in Minase / Kumono-Nagareyama House

33 House type
Townh. in Daita / House in Nago / House in Sakatayamatsuke / House in Imajuku / Common H. in Sanda / House in Soshigaya

65 Independent structure and diffused border
Project KO / Project S / House F

77 Openness towards the city
Common City Hoshida / Kumamoto Takuma Housing / Housing in Makuhari Baytown

95 The release of architecture
House SA / Hut T / QUICO Jingumae

117 Small compact unit and island plan
Egota House / Werkbundsiedlung Wiesenfeld / Munich 2018 Winter Olympic Village

135 Composition in tension with reality
Tokyo Tech Front / Amitsu Primary School

151 Opening of the closed box
Minase Annex / House in Sanda Renovation

163 The liberated ordinary space
Conclusion

171 Freedom to think architecture
Go Hasegawa

177 Appendix
Biography / Bibliography / Catalogue of works

まえがき

ベアロッハー太央、サミュエル・スカッサビア

本書は坂本一成氏が2013年12月にスイスのメンドリジオ建築アカデミーで行った講演をきっかけに生まれました。この講演は私達がアシスタントを務めた長谷川豪客員教授の設計スタジオで開催されたものです。当時の講演を体験して頂くために、その内容を本書に忠実に再現させました。

この講演では初期から今日までの作品が紹介されると共に、坂本氏の思想の進化の歩みも明示されています。氏は常に建築の理論と実践を追及してきた建築家であることから、言葉とイメージを併せ持つ講演という形式によって理論と実践の両方を本書では紹介することができると考えました。講演の内容を区切る各章は建築のテーマであると同時に、現代の空間を常に追い求め続ける坂本氏の姿勢の変遷も示しています。

坂本氏は自身の作品をとおして現実と建築のあらたな関係性を問う議論を切り開きました。この継続性のある議論は今日の建築を考える上で重要な意味を持つと私達は考えます。それは現実との関係を築きながら、同時にその枠組みから自由でいられる建築の可能性を追求することであります。坂本一成氏は私たちの断片化した社会のなかで、現実と建築のあらたな結びつきを追求し、築くことによって、建築の孤立を避けると同時に自立性を確保することを可能とする建築の進歩を暗示しているように思われます。

Foreword
Tao Baerlocher, Samuele Squassabia

This publication arises from a lecture that Kazunari Sakamoto held at the Accademia di Architettura di Mendrisio in December 2013. The lecture took place in the design studio of the Visiting Professor Go Hasegawa, where we were both working as teaching assistants. With the intention to present the content in its original form, we transcribed the lecture directly on paper in this book.
The lecture includes works from the beginning of his career until today and discloses the evolution of his thinking. Sakamoto is equally engaged in the fields of theory and practice and the format of the lecture with words and images allows him to present both aspects simultaneously. We structured the content in chapters, expressing the themes of his work and manifesting his constant search for contemporary space in architecture.
Sakamoto opened a discourse concerning the question of a new relationship between architecture and reality, which is not yet concluded. We believe that this question is of great importance in today's discussion. Throughout his work, he explores how architecture can include reality and yet be released from its restrictions at the same time. Within the fragmentation of our world, he strives to establish new connections, showing a possibility for an evolution in which architecture will avoid isolation and achieve autonomy.

講演
坂本一成

Lecture
Kazunari Sakamoto

自由な空間を求めて

The search for the free space

私の設計した建物は日本でも理解しがたい建築と言われますが、その理由の多くは私の建物に強い表現がない事に拠ると思います。つまり私の造ってきたものは、強いあるいは特異な形態を持ったイメージ的な建築ではありませんし、豪快でダイナミックな、またヒロイックな建築ではありません。更に人々に対し昂揚感を与えるクライマックスを持つ建物でもありません。
そうした強い表現の空間、あるいは特異といえる空間のなかにリアリティーを私自身感じないのです。よりなんでもない、あたりまえの普通さの中に、まさにオーディナリーな日常的な世界と連続する所にこそ私にとってのリアリティーある現代の私たちの空間があると考えてきました。それは私が対象としてきた空間の多くが、日常的空間である住宅であったことも大きな理由でありましょう。

My architecture is said to be difficult to understand in Japan. I think the biggest reason is there is no strong expression in my designs. Houses I have completed are not image-based buildings with strong or unique forms; neither being magnificent, nor dynamic, nor heroic architecture. Also my buildings do not have a climax that gives people a strong elevated emotional effect.
I myself do not feel reality in a space that is strongly or uniquely expressed. I believed our realistic contemporary space exists in the common ordinariness, in a place that is continuous with the world of everyday life. Furthermore, the most subjects I have been focusing on are residences, which have space for everyday life.

私が求めてきたものは、自由で、豊かな、そして柔らかな空間です。こうした日常的な空間を求めるために様々な建物の構成に関する操作をしたわけです。今日はそのことを中心にお話ししますが、その操作とは主として様々な水準で建築にまとわりつく類型的構成に関する操作であり、その操作の結果がもたらすものは、紋切り型化した世界を解放する空間であります。
つまり、建築が建築ゆえの性格として持つ閉鎖系の空間をいかに開いて開放系の空間にしようとするかをお話ししようと思います。そのことは結局ある種の「建築」という制度からの解放であり、そうした建築という枠組みがつくりだした様々な規制から自由になることであろうと思われます。

それでは早速、私の仕事を見ていただきます。

The space I have been seeking for is free, diverse and soft. In order to achieve such ordinary space, I have been operating with the aspect of composition in various buildings. My lecture today is mainly about this operation, which deals with the typological composition appearing on various levels in architecture. The result of this operation leads to a space, which liberates the fixed and formalised world.
So I would like to explain how I tried to open the closed space of architecture, which is due to its own nature, in order to create a space with an open character. After all, I feel this is a kind of release from the institution called 'architecture' and a liberation from the various restrictions born out of the architectural framework.

Well then I would like to start my presentation.

閉じた箱

The closed box

18　散田の家

1969年に竣工した私の最初の住宅です。設計に際し「現代の自由を与える空間は閉じた箱」だと直感し、その事を表現したと言えますが、同時にその「閉じた箱」は建物を纏める統合の仕方を意味します。大きな閉じた世界、つまり自由な広がりのある空間にコスモスをつくるということが最初のイメージですが、このイメージは、条件が許す範囲での大空間をつくって、その中に機能的な場所を小箱として入れるというボックス・イン・ボックスの配列で構成されています。このことは、建物によって地上の空間的広がりを小さく区切るということで狭い空間とならざるを得ないのに対して、広がりを確保するという矛盾であることを意味します。

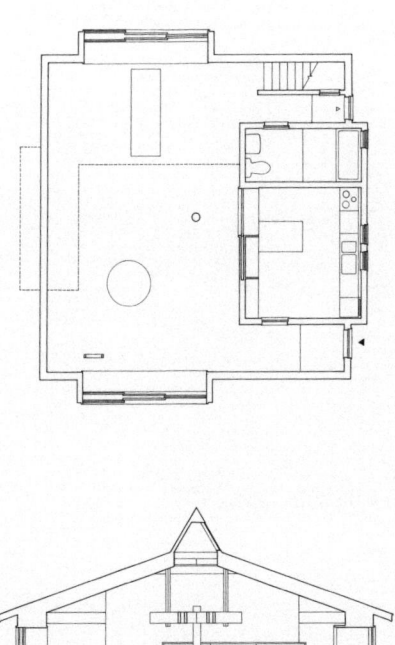

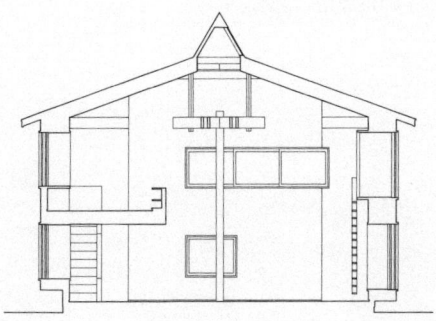

1階平面図 + 断面図 / Ground floor + Section / 1:200

This was my first work completed in 1969. The house expresses my intuition felt on designing at that time; the space to give freedom is the 'closed box'. At the same time this closed box means a method to bring the building to a unity. A big closed universe, namely the creation of a cosmos inside a free and expanding space was the first image. This image is composed by creating a room as big as conditions permit and by disposing functional places as small boxes in an arrangement called 'box in a box'. The aim of this composition to create expansion means a contradiction, since a building unavoidably divides the spatial surface of the site into smaller spaces.

またこの住宅では、この包含関係による構成と、正方形の平面や中心の柱をともなうラショナルな構成と重なって、中心性の強い完結的な空間を形成していると思います。その後、より空間を解放化するために、こうした中心性を伴った完結的空間を避けること、また「閉じた箱」を相対化して開放的空間とすることが強くなります。しかしこの住宅でも、障子で視覚的に閉じているとはいえ、南側と北側の2面で大きな開口をとり外部に対して開放的にしています。つまり、この「閉じた箱」も開きながら閉じるという相反的で両義性な空間となっていることがわかると思います。

I also think that the composition based on the relationship of inclusion and the rational composition with the square floor plan and the central column overlap to form a kind of complete space with a strong centre point. With the aim to release the space, I later started to avoid this kind of complete space with centrality and began to relativise the closed box towards a space with an open character. Although this house is visually closed by the paper sliding doors, it has an open character towards the outside by designing big openings on the south and the north side. Consequently this closed box creates both contradictory and ambiguous space in closing as well as opening.

24　水無瀬の町家

　これは翌年、1970年にできました「水無瀬の町家」といいます。街の中にあることに積極的に対応したという意味で町家と呼んでいます。この建物も包含関係であるボックス・イン・ボックス的空間配列をもっていますが、包含された小箱が多いことから空間的な結びつきの関係はより複雑で有機的になっていると思います。街道的な前面道路に向かって、それなりの大きさの窓がありますが、内部空間にこれらの窓が開口として積極的に生かされてはいません。そういう意味では「閉じた箱」となっているわけですが、町家と称しているように街に連続した形態、構成によって完結した構成が避けられていることが理解されると思います。

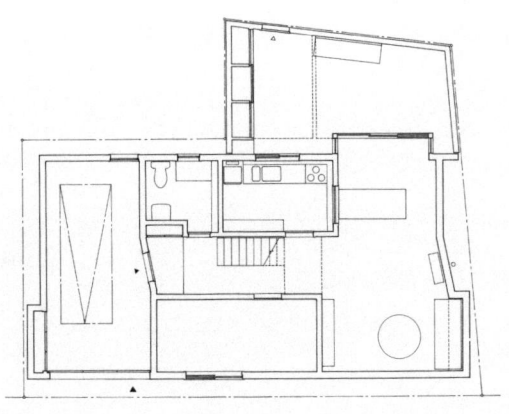

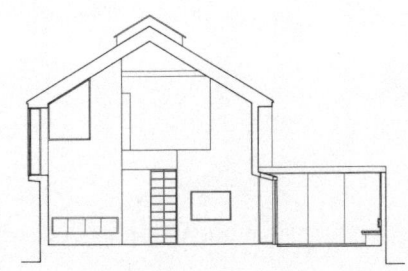

1階平面図 + 断面図 / Ground floor + Section / 1:200

This house, called Townhouse in Minase, was completed the following year in 1970. I called it a townhouse, as it actively reacts to the fact that it stood in town. The building also has the spatial arrangement of a box in a box, with the relationship of inclusion. As there are many small boxes included, the relationship between the spaces becomes more complex and organic. There are considerable windows facing the front road, which has the character of a main street. However those windows are not actively utilized as openings in the interior space. Referring to this fact, the house is a closed box. But as it is called townhouse, the form and the composition create continuity towards the town, avoiding a closed and complete composition.

26　水無瀬の町家

この建物は壁までRCで、その上に木造の切妻屋根が架かっています。「閉じた箱」の建物ではありますが、単純な切妻屋根が架かっていることから、その後の「家型」の住宅の萌芽があると見ることも出来ます。また建物の外形が平屋ではなく、かといって2層分とも言えぬ中間的な曖昧なスケールであることに気付かれると思いますが、このことで建物の形でありながら平屋建て、あるいは2階建てという建物の類型的形態であることが避けられていることがわかります。これ以降の建物にもこうしたスケール感のものが度々現れます。

Townhouse in Minase

In this building, reinforced concrete is used for the walls and floors, while the gable roof is in wood. The building is a closed box, but the simple gable roof can be understood as an initial seed of a house-type residence that will appear later. You may also notice the ambiguous scale of the exterior form, neither belonging to a single nor a two-storey house. Although the residence has the shape of a building, it avoids having the typological form of a single or two-storey building. The scale with such characteristics will appear from time to time in my later buildings.

28 　雲野流山の家

1973年竣工のこの住宅では、物質感、素材感を完全に消すことはせず、コンクリートの打ち放しの壁やスラブの素材を活かしながら、白、あるいはシルバー色に塗ることで、一次的・直接的な材料の持つ表面の性格を消して、その裏側にある物質性は残しています。このことから、抽象的でありながら具体性を伴った空間であり、曖昧な宙吊り化した物質感による意味の消去と言えます。

Kumono-Nagareyama House

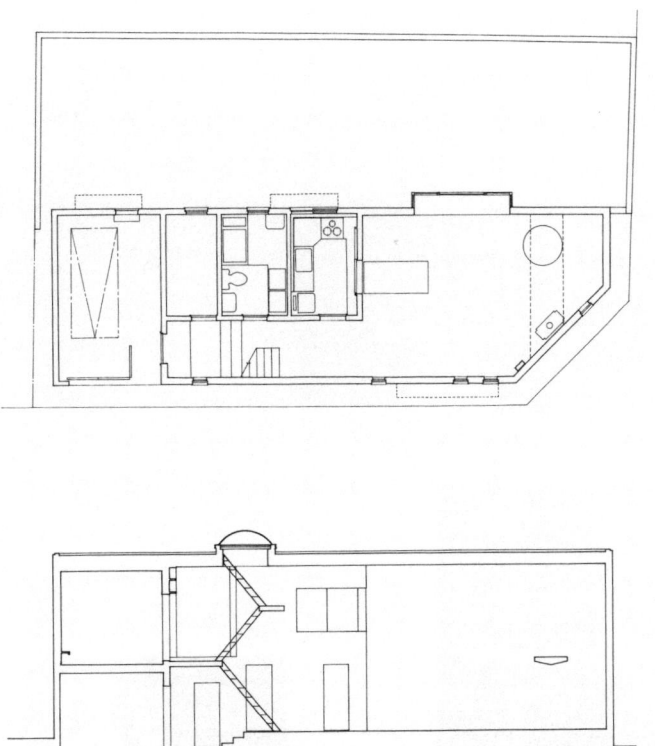

1階平面図 + 断面図 / Ground floor + Section / 1:200

This house was completed in 1973. Without completely erasing the texture and materiality, I painted the naked concrete walls and ceiling in either white or silver colour. I wiped off the primary and direct character of the material surface while keeping and using the materiality behind it. In this way, the space becomes both abstract and concrete and we can say that the ambiguous and suspended feeling of the material leads to the elimination of its meaning.

この建物はフラットルーフの直方体的形態をもちますが、幾何学的でありながら敷地形状にそって建物の形状が削がれているといった合理性に関する矛盾を内包しています。この建物の主室の幅は4.5m、天井高も4.5mと正方形の断面ですが、長方形方面の隅部が削がれてやや垂直性をもった空間となるところを途中で幅狭い水面スラブ材を与えることで安定を保つという、バランスを形成しています。

This building has a rectangular form with a flat roof, but as the geometrical form is sliced off along the perimeter of the site, the building includes a contradiction in rationality. While the main space has a square section with a 4.5 m width and ceiling height, the cut in the corner creates a slightly vertical space, whereby a thin horizontal slab in the middle restores the balance and stability.

家型

House type

34　代田の町家

次は「代田の町家」、1976年です。この住宅も閉鎖的ではありますが、同時に前面道路に積極的に連続させるなど地域環境に開こうとしている相反的関係が見られます。この住宅ではボックス・イン・ボックスの空間から脱却して、内部空間の包含関係はありません。部屋どうしが平面的に接触する隣接関係となるプランニングとなっています。また木造で勾配屋根であり、正面側が切妻です。このことから家型というアノニマスな建築の統合の形態を意識することになり、この「家型」と呼ぶ切妻型の住宅がこの後、続くことになります。また木造故に持っている柔らかさ、軽さに親近感をもちました。

Townhouse in Daita 35

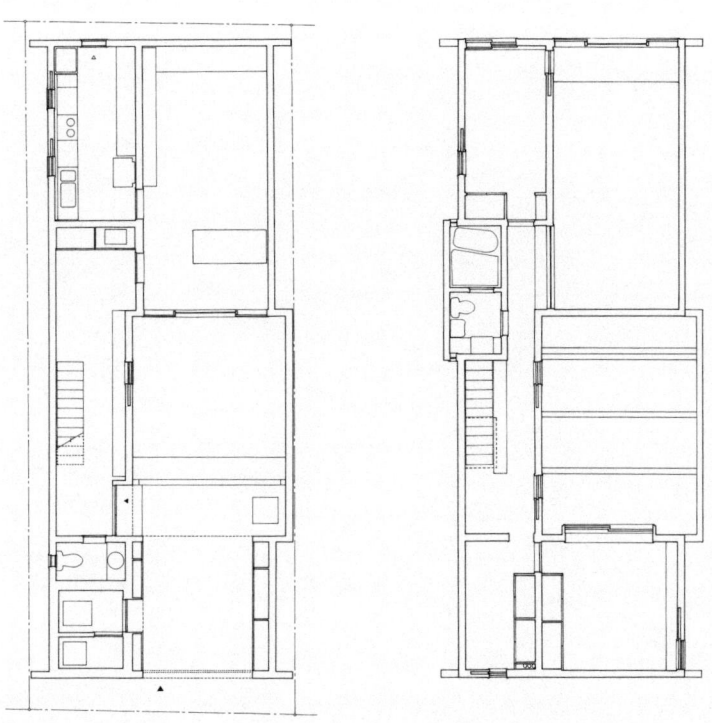

1階 + 2階平面図 / Ground floor + 1. floor / 1:200

This Townhouse in Daita was completed in 1976. The house also has a closed character, but as it actively connects to the front road and opens towards the surrounding at the same time, we discover a contradictory relationship. The house has moved away from the arrangement of a box in a box and there is no relationship of inclusion in the interior space. Here the rooms are juxtaposed horizontally in plan and are arranged in a relationship of adjacency. It is a wooden construction with a pitched roof and a front-side gable. Since then I became conscious of the so-called 'house type' as a form of unity in anonymous architecture. Houses with a gable roof as a house type will continue to appear later. I also felt an affinity towards the lightness and softness of wooden construction.

ところで一般的に住宅では、居間とか寝室とかいったプログラムに対応して想定される部屋名を付けます。確かにそこに住まわれる方のための生活のプログラムに対応するためのネーミングの必要もありますが、それと共に私の建築の空間的構成の見地からは別の違った表現が必要となってくるわけです。そのことから部屋を建物内部の空間構成の関係を示す内容として、「室」、「主室」というように、また部屋と部屋を結ぶところを「間室」として空間配列の関係を示す室名としました。中庭も「外室」という言い方で、建築のプランニングを即物的な室の配列の中に位置づけようとしました。

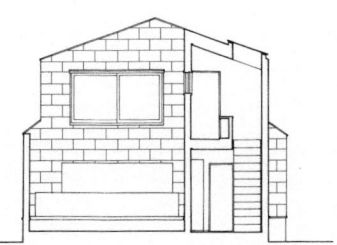

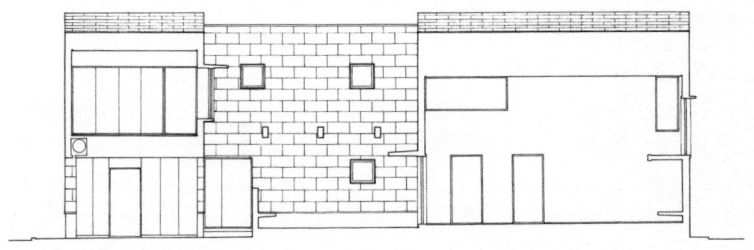

東西方向断面図 + 南北方向断面図 / Cross section + Long section / 1:200

By the way, we generally name rooms like the living room or bedroom according to the assumed programme in the house. Certainly it is necessary to name rooms that correspond to the programme of the resident's lifestyle, but at the same time there is a need for another description of space regarding the spatial composition in my architecture. Therefore I named the spaces to indicate the relationship of the spatial composition inside my building. The rooms are called 'room', 'main-room' or the connection between rooms 'interval-room', indicating the relationship of the spatial arrangement. Also by calling the inner court an 'exterior-room', I tried to treat the architectural planning as an objective arrangement of rooms.

この1階の「間室」は主室と外室、そして2階の2つの室を結びつける結節のための部屋です。これ以前の「散田の家」、「水無瀬の町家」、「雲野流山の家」では、主室に包含されていたこの結節の部分が独立して室化したことを意味します。まさに隣接関係で構成されたプランニングの象徴的な室です。「外室」は室化した中庭です。ここは中庭という外部であり、また室という内部化した場所という矛盾した二重の意味を内包した空間です。この「外室」は主室ともうひとつの外室の間に位置し、両者を結びつける役割も担っております。

Townhouse in Daita 41

The interval-room on the ground floor is a space to connect the main-room and the exterior-room, as well as the two rooms on the upper floor. The connecting area, which was part of the main room in the previous houses in Sanda, Minase and Nagareyama, has become an independent room. This room is symbolic of the plan based on the relationship of adjacency. The exterior-room is a courtyard with the character of a room. Since it is an outside courtyard and yet inside a room, the space combines two contrasting meanings. Furthermore this exterior-room is placed between the main-room and another exterior-room with the function of connecting these two spaces.

42　南湖の家

これは「南湖の家」、1976年の設計で1978年に竣工しました。この建物は、切妻の屋根で覆われた大きなワンルーム的な内部空間が細かく分節された部分をもつ構成です。この内部は壁面全体に広がった棚を始め様々な建築化した家具で細かく分節されていますが、それらと天井、床等と全ての内部構成材はラワンベニヤ材で統一されています。このことはこの空間が部位毎に分節されている一方、同一の仕上げによって全体が統合されているという相反的な両義性を有していることを意味します。また壁であり棚であるという両義的な性格をもたらしています。

House in Nago   43

This house in Nago was designed in 1976 and completed in 1978. The building is composed of a large, single interior space with a gabled roof and finely segmented parts. The interior space is segmented by various furniture that become architectural elements, like the shelf along the entire wall. Furthermore, all components of the interior space, like the furniture, ceiling and floor, are unified with the same plywood material. The articulation of space in each element on the one hand, and the unification of the whole through the same finish on the other hand, leads to a contradicting ambiguity. It also produces the ambiguous character of being a wall and a shelf at the same time.

こうしたなかで、動線に沿って切り妻の天井の長手方向が対応し、また家具が全部その方向に対して平行に配置されています。とくに大きなテーブルは更に対立したスケールを伴って象徴化されております。この様に全体としては切妻屋根による家型という形のうちに全体が統合されているのです。またこの建物では外室と呼んだ囲まれた屋外スペースを内部とは対立的に設けて、建物全体の纏まりを複合的に構成しています。

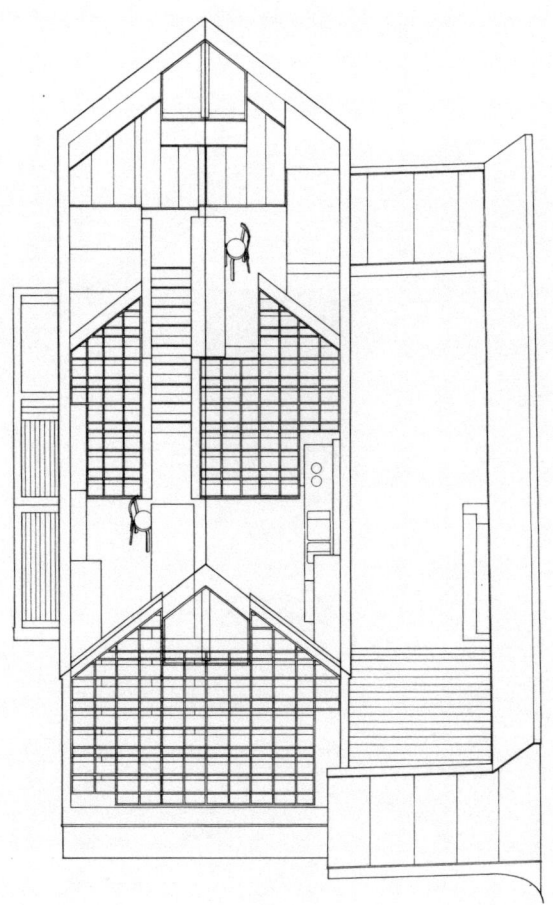

アクソノメトリック / Axonometry

In all this, the longitudinal direction of the gable roof corresponds to the movement of circulation and also all furniture is placed parallel to it. Especially the big table receives a symbolic meaning by having a contrasting scale. The whole building is therefore brought to a unity within the form of the gabled roof as house type. Further by placing an enclosed exterior-room in contrast to the interior space, the whole building is ordered in a multilayered composition.

46 坂田山附の家

この建物は1978年に竣工した切妻屋根の妻入り側を正面とした典型的な家型の住宅です。1.5層分の高さの軒高で、曖昧なスケールとプロポーションの建物です。主室を上階にワンルームで配置し、いくつかの室を下階に隣接関係に配置する構成です。この住宅は普通の建物のようでありながら、窓の位置や形状によって普通のあり方とはやや異なる建物になっていると思います。

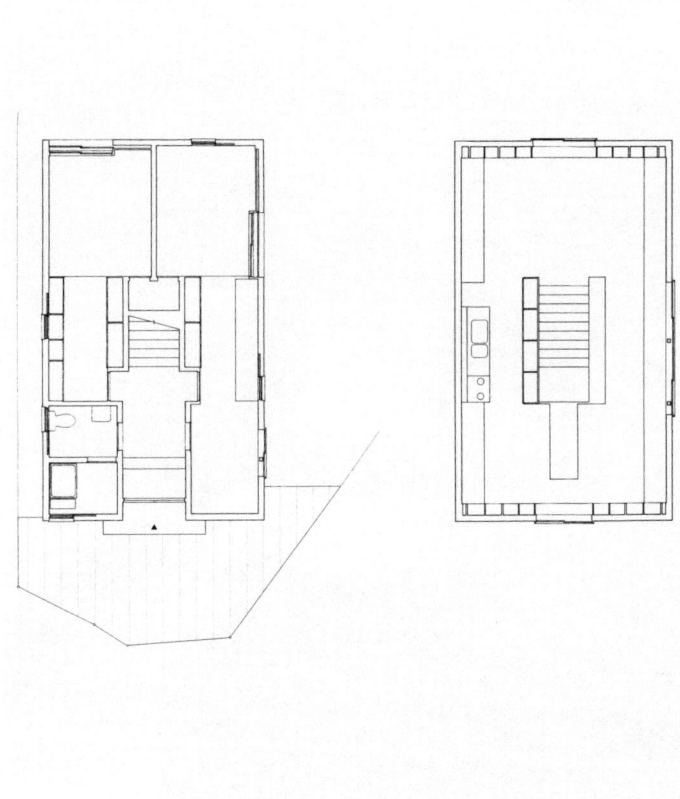

1階 + 2階平面図 / Ground floor + 1. floor / 1:200

This is a typical house type residence built in 1978 with the gable on the front side. The building has an ambiguous scale and proportion with the eaves height at 1.5 stories. The composition consists of a single space as a main room on the upper floor and several rooms in the relationship of adjacency on the ground floor. It seems to be a normal building, but the form of the building and the position of the window create a subtle difference to the ordinary buildings.

上階のワンルームは主室としての広がりを持ちながら高さ方向では屋根裏部屋的スケールとプロポーションをもっています。また壁部において軸組の構造体と表皮が独立して配置されています。このことから、開口部である窓に柱材が露出することになりました。これらのことから、この建物は複数の異なる文脈の集合によって形成されていることが分かります。そして、それを成立させているのは主として構成の重合によるレトリックによることが理解されると思います。

House in Sakatayamatsuke

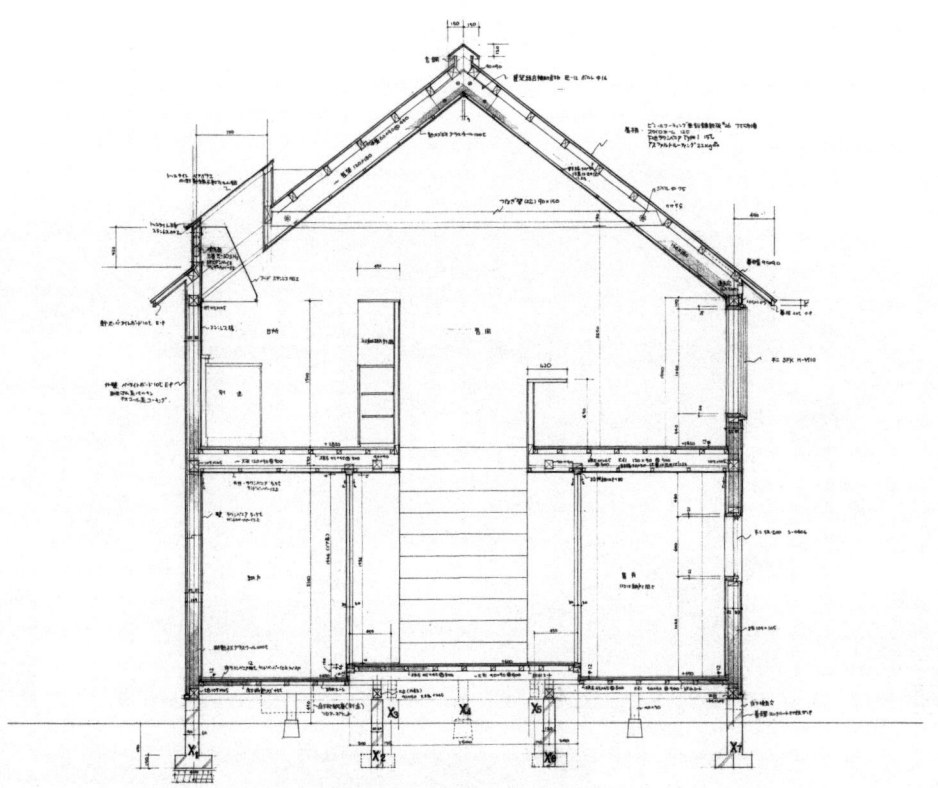

断面詳細図 / Detail section / 1:75

The single space on the upper floor has the size of a main room, but in its height it has the scale and proportion of an attic space. Further on the wall, the structural elements of the frame construction and the envelope are arranged independently and the column is exposed through the window opening. Accordingly, the building is formulated by integrating different contexts. You can understand that this is mainly achieved through the rhetoric of layered compositions.

これができたのは同じ1978年、「今宿の家」と呼んでいます。日本でのいわゆるポストモダンの時代に入った時の建物です。そういう意味でかなりマニエリスティックになっています。この建物の窓などの開口の取り方を見るともう閉じた箱ではないことがお分かりになると思います。また外形を周りの地域に晒した建物の形態が表現的になっております。外形は家型を基本としており軒側に下屋的な張りが出現し、家型のバリエーションを示しています。

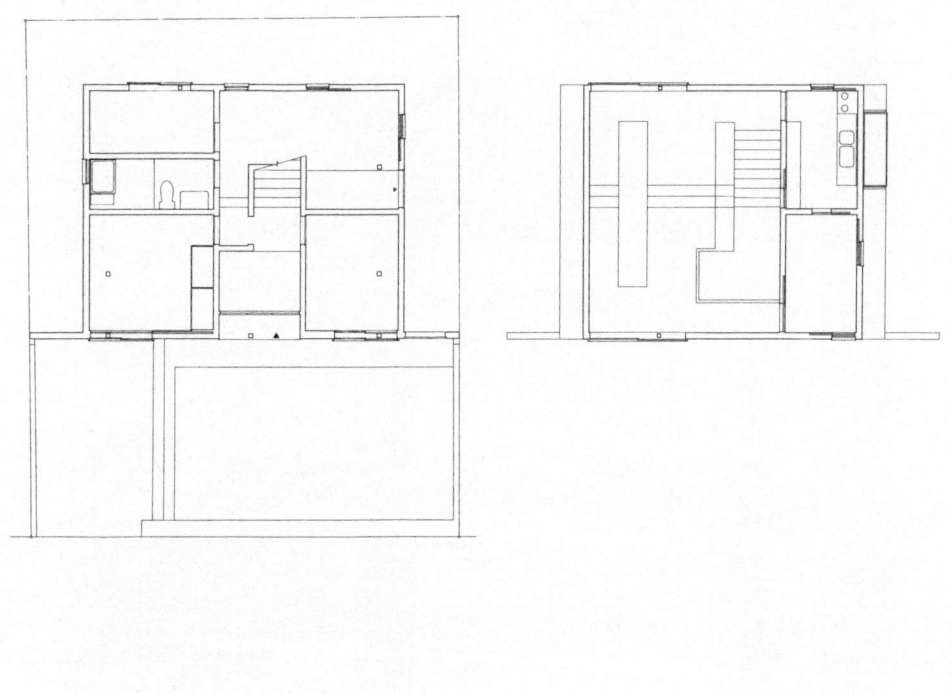

1階 + 2階平面図 / Ground floor + 1. floor / 1:200

This house in Imajuku was erected in the same year in 1978. It was built when postmodernism began in Japan and consequently it includes aspects of mannerism. You can see from the window openings that the house is no longer an expression of the closed box. Furthermore, the exposure of the external form towards the surroundings is significant for the expression of this building. The external form is based on the house type, yet with the enlargement resembling a lean-to on the eaves side, it represents a variation of the house type.

またこれだけの大きな屋根をつくりながら上階の主室の天井は軒高で水平です。形態の秩序と内部空間は一致してなく、複眼的関係を形成しています。こうしたことはこの建物が形態の操作に拠ったものであることがわかると思います。また開口部に柱材が前作に比べ、より積極的に露出しており、架構と表層がより明確に分離されていることがわかります。

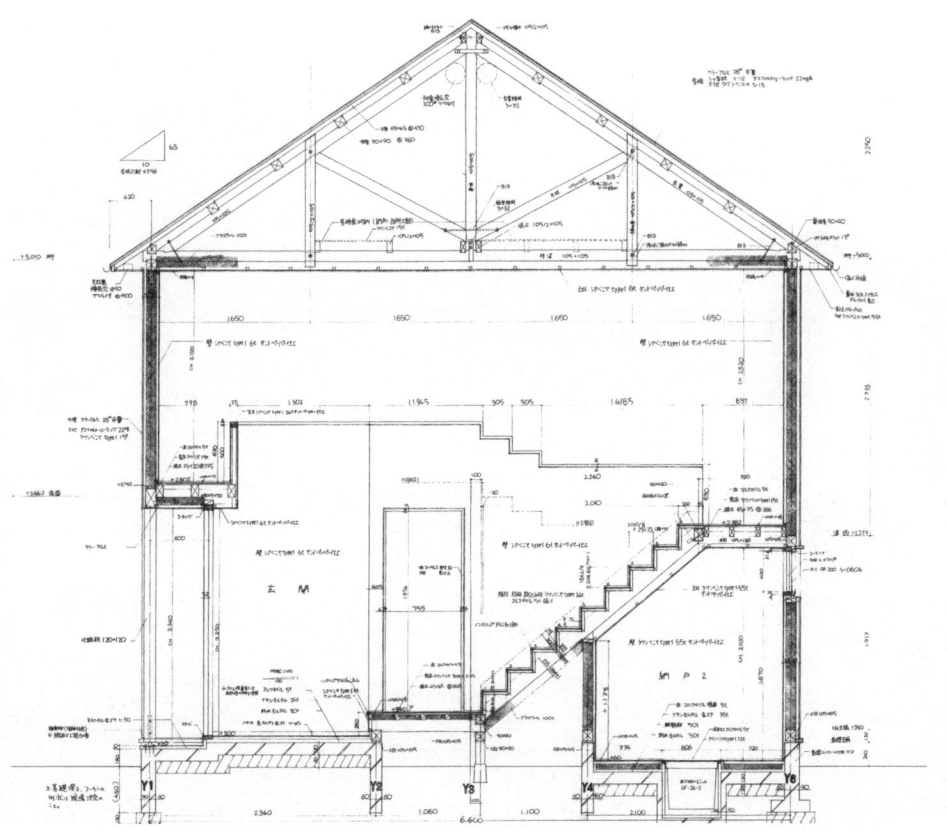

断面詳細図 / Detail section / 1:75

In spite of creating such a big roof, the main room on the upper floor has a flat ceiling at the height of the eaves. The logic of the form and the interior space is not mutually coherent, creating a relationship of multiple viewpoints. You can see that this is due to the operation on the form of the building. The columns are more actively exposed than in the previous project and we can recognise a clear separation between the structure and the envelope.

54　散田の共同住宅

これは1980年に竣工した、戸建の住宅ではなく学生のための10戸のアパートです。中庭があって、そこから各戸に分かれた入り口と結ばれています。家型の組み合わせと見ることができます。前の建物と同様に柱が窓に出ているのが分かると思います。一般には窓に柱を露出させることなく調整するわけです。ここではそうではなく全体の架構を自立させ、そこに自由に窓をつける方法によっています。こういうことで架構と表皮という二重性による展開ができるのではないかと考えたわけです。

Common House in Sanda   55

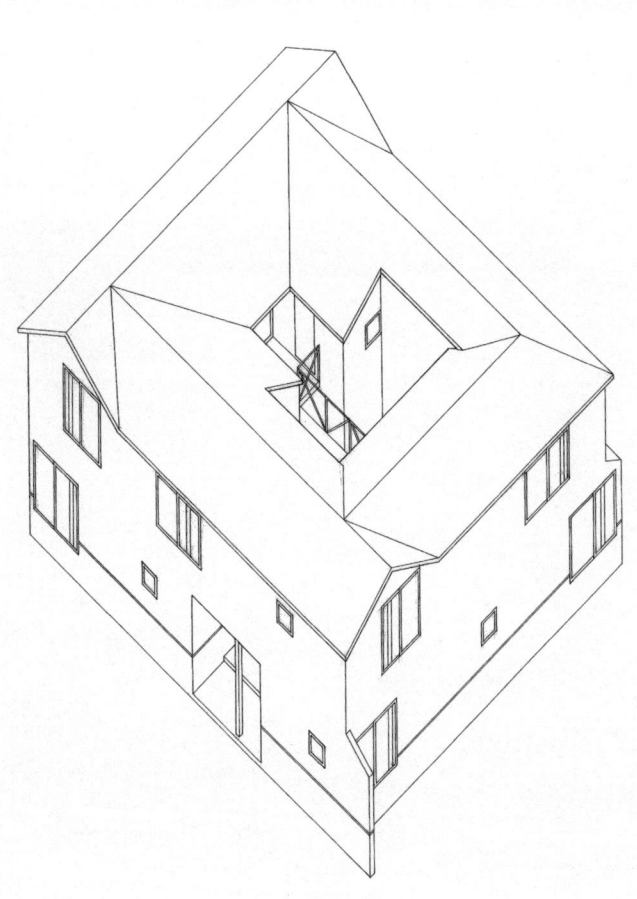

アクソノメトリック / Axonometry

This house from 1980 is not a single residence, but includes ten apartment units for students. The building has a courtyard that provides access to each unit and it can be seen as a combination of the house types. You may notice the exposed columns in the windows as in the previous buildings. Usually we arrange them without exposing the columns in windows. Here on the contrary, I treated the whole structure independently and placed the windows freely beside them. In this way, I hoped to unfold the duality of the column and the envelope.

56　散田の共同住宅

切妻屋根4棟を口の字形に組み合わせ、その中央部に残った外部空間を外室として、そこから内部空間を経ないで各戸にアプローチする計画となっています。このことはコモンスペースを内部化することなく、外部のパブリックスペースに連続させる、その後のスモール・コンパクト・ユニットとアイランド・プランの先がけとなった計画と言えます。

The four gabled roof buildings are arranged around the central exterior-room, which provides direct access to each unit without passing through the interior space. This common space is not planned as an interior space, but in continuity with the exterior public space and can be understood as a precursor of the small compact unit and island plan I will turn to later.

祖師谷の家

1981年の仕事です。部屋数の多い住宅で、室の隣接関係によるつくり方で全体が構成されています。この屋根は三角柱。半ヴォールト、そして三角柱の奥はまたヴォールトとなっています。こういう説明から幾何学形態のボリュームによる構成だと見えるかも知れません。しかし、このファサードを見ていただくと、このファサードは切妻のブロークン・ペディメントとなっているとも言えます。このことは家型と幾何学的な構成とを絡ませた形態操作による両義的な結果と言えます。

House in Soshigaya

This work was completed in 1981. The residence contains many rooms and the spatial composition is based on the relationship of adjacency. A triangular prism, a half-vault and another vault behind the triangular prism form the roof. Through this explanation one may see a composition of volumes with geometrical forms. However you may notice that the façade can also be seen as a broken pediment of the gabled roof. This ambiguity is a result of the operation on form, in which the house type and the composition with geometrical forms are combined.

この住宅の主室は、腰から上の覆い側と下の床側とに仕上げを変え、空間を分節しています。この操作を建物全体に貫くことで建物全体を纏めています。つまり、この建物では並列的な多くの室の配列によって内部空間を分節し、逆に各室の仕上げを腰で分ける事によってそれらの部屋の空間的連続性をつくっています。形態操作の強い作品となっています。このように、この住宅は1970年代後半の日本のポストモダニズム風潮に少なからず影響を受けて、装飾的な趣きを伴った作品と言えます。

1階平面図 + 断面図 / Ground floor + Section / 1:200

I divided the main room of this house along its waistline between the upper ceiling half and the lower floor half with a different finish. By persisting with the same method all over the house, the whole building is unified. The aligned arrangement of multiple rooms divides the interior space, but the different finish along the waistline creates a spatial continuity among the rooms. It is a work with a strong operation on the form. This house is considerably influenced by the movement of postmodernism in Japan during the late 1970s and accordingly it features an ornamental appearance.

自由な架構と広がりの領域

Independent structure and diffused border

生活する場、空間そのものを素朴に即物的に提出できないだろうか。建物は一つの覆いですから、天井の高さが自由にとれるような覆いで良いのではないか。それをサポートする柱も必要ならばそれなりに並べればいいのではないか。装飾的、操作的な意味からの建築ではなく、より即物的なものにしたいと意識した計画です。これは実現できずプロジェクトで終わったのですが、私にとって大きく方向を変更した重要なプロジェクトです。つまり家型という文脈で纏めたものではなく、平面的広がりのなかで完結した全体性を放棄したあり方を求めたもので、もっと即物的な機能的な処理の仕方で建築ができないだろうかということを考えた計画でした。

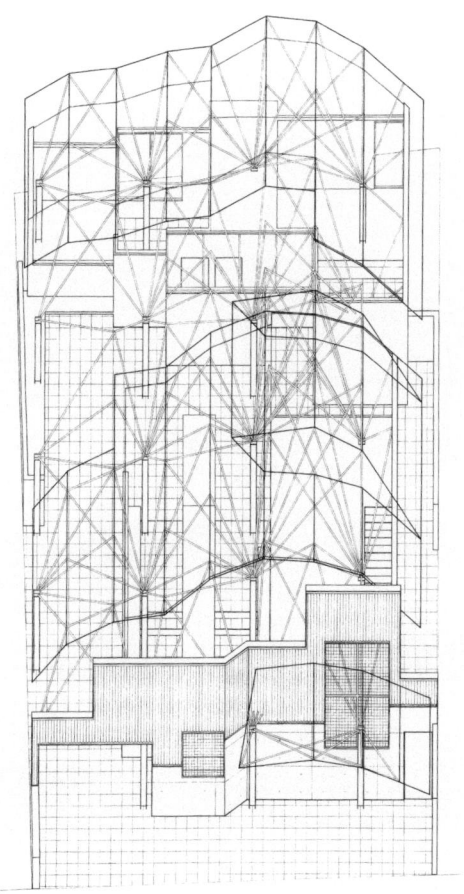

アクソノメトリック / Axonometry

Would it be possible to express the living place or the space itself in a natural and objective way? Since a building is a kind of cover, could it be a cover with flexible ceiling heights? Couldn't we place supporting columns according to necessity? In this project I hoped to create architecture in an objective and direct way, which could be free from decorative or rhetorical meanings. This project didn't ever materialise, but still became important in providing me with a major turning point. The project is no longer settled in the context of the house type, but sought existence in abandoning the complete wholeness in favour of the horizontal expansion. In this design I intended to create architecture by treating it in a more objective and functional manner.

1986年に日本の住宅メーカーの依頼で設計した住宅の計画案です。量産化が困難との理由で実現できませんでした。この計画では自由な架構と場による空間構成を目指しました。敷地全体に生活行為に対応した場がより自由に展開され、さらにその場を自由に覆うことによって内部と外部の区別が曖昧化して、更にそれぞれの室やそれぞれの場が緩やかに連結してやわらかな空間が形成されるよう試みました。

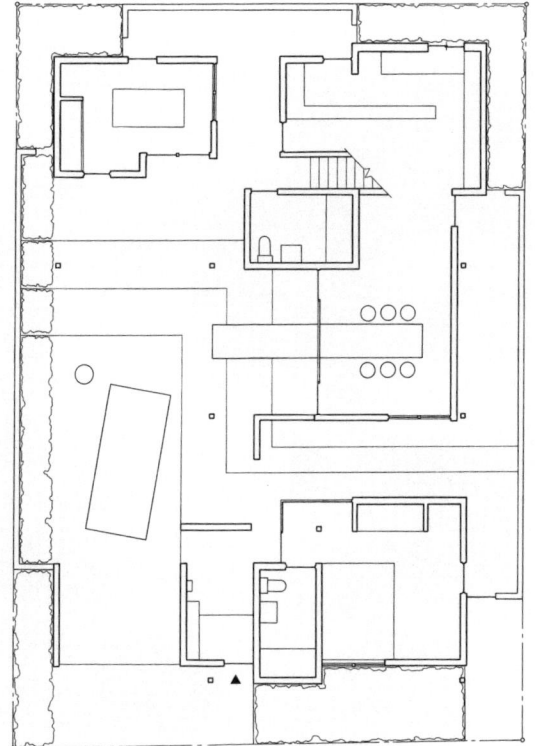

1階平面図 / Ground floor / 1:200

This is a project on behalf of a Japanese housing company in 1986. It couldn't be built due to difficulties for mass production. In this project I aimed for the spatial composition that is based on independent structure and open places. Various places corresponding to living activities are spread freely across the entire site. Also, by covering them loosely, the distinction between inside and outside becomes ambiguous. It was my intention to establish a smooth connection between each room and place, in order to create a space that is soft and diffuse.

こうした考えが実現したのが「House F」です。1988年です。グリッド状に配列された柱から連続した斜め材によって折板状の屋根を支えることで架構が成立しています。このことにより自由な高さの空間が確保されます。プランニングは、包含関係を部分的に含んで隣接関係で展開する計画となっております。片側には寝室である室が3つ重なり、コンクリートの箱になっています。このように特定な架構法で全体が纏まるのではなく、架構方法の違いから全体が分節されています。

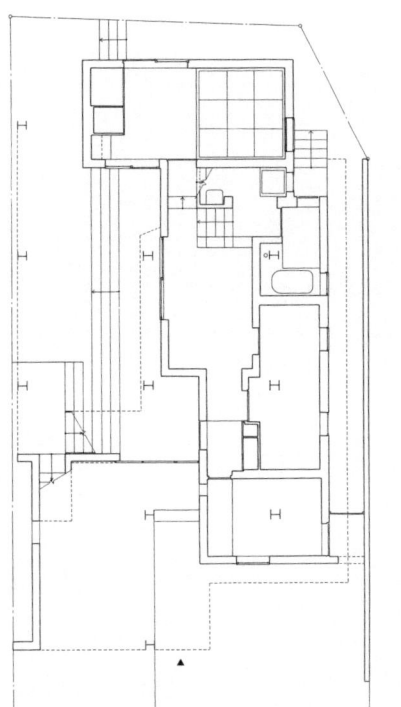
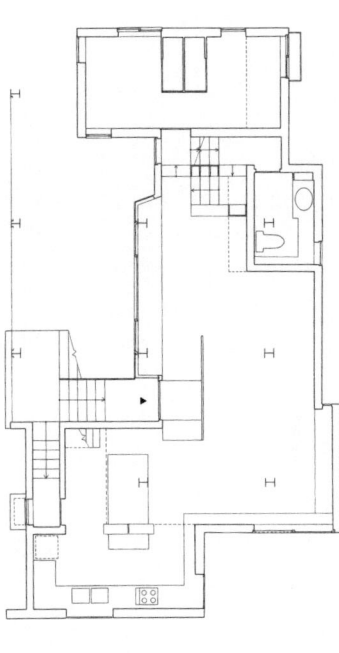

1階 + 2階平面図 / Ground floor + 1. floor / 1:200

I could carry out my idea in House F in 1988. Columns arranged in a grid form with outgrowing inclined elements support the folded panel roof and compose the structure. Consequently a space with a flexible ceiling height is achieved. The planning is based on the relationship of adjacency and partly includes the relationship of inclusion. On one side three bedrooms are stacked in the form of a concrete box. The whole is therefore not unified by a particular structure, but rather subdivided by different kinds of structure.

また初期の作品と違って、4面のエレベーションが違っています。それはある意味で完結性が崩れてきて建物が断片化したと言えるかと思います。この建物は床のレベルが11ほどに分かれています。そういう意味では室というより断片化された場の連続、組み合わせで全体ができていると言えます。このように、この建物では「自由な架構と広がりの領域」を実現し、様々な高さの床が場所に応じて設定され、壁も天井まで達せず必要な高さで領域を区切る構成となっています。

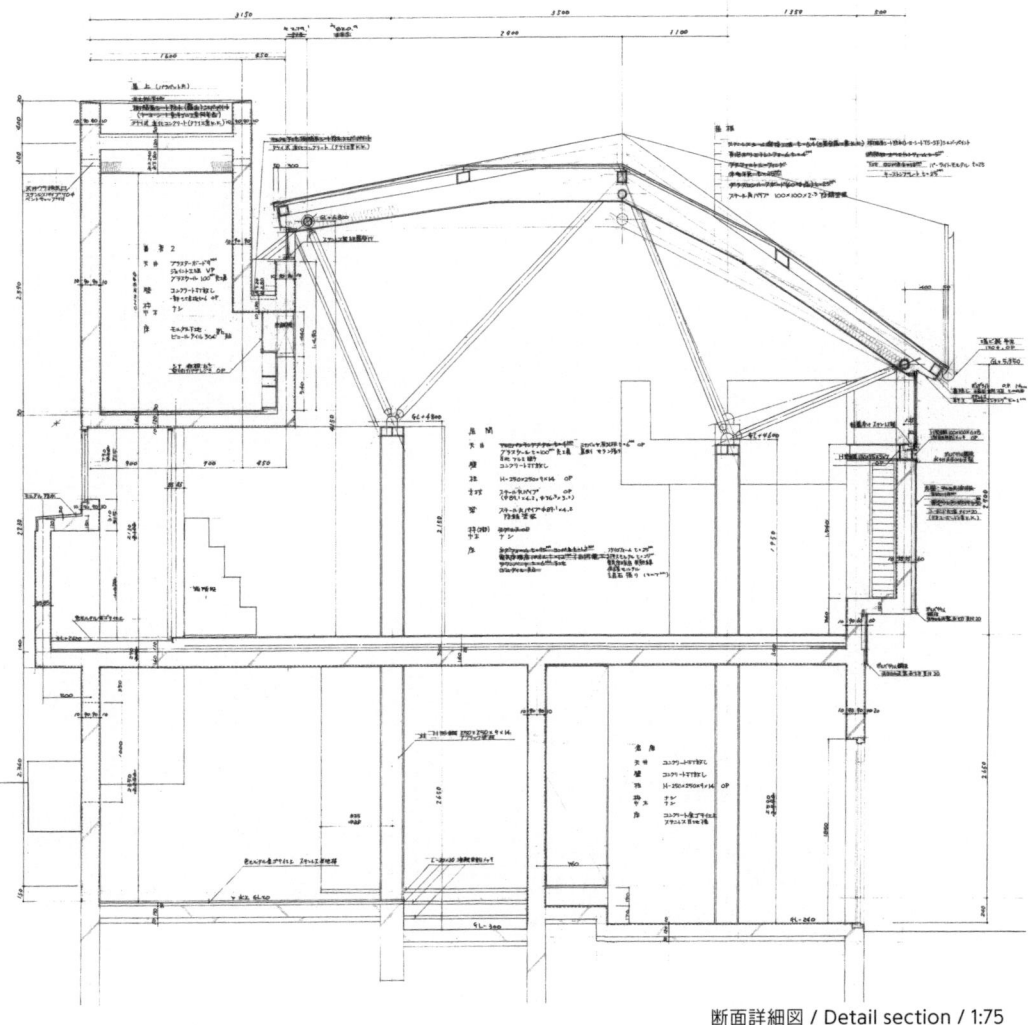

断面詳細図 / Detail section / 1:75

Unlike my earlier works, all four elevations are different. We can say the completeness has disintegrated and the building has become more fragmented. The floor of this house is separated into eleven levels. Considering this fact, the whole building is made by the connection and continuity of fragmented places instead of rooms. In this composition, different floor levels are defined according to each place and walls with only the necessary height limit the space without reaching the ceiling. The 'independent structure and diffused border' was finally achieved.

都市への開放

Openness towards the city

「House F」のようなものを112戸、それに集会所を加えてそれらを敷地全体に散在させた計画と言えます。ここで一番重要なことはスロープ造成にしたことです。この土地は十分の一ぐらいの勾配があります。普通日本では、こうした傾斜地は住宅地にするために雛壇状に造成します。このプロジェクトでは、連続して広がる大地に住宅をばらまいたような形にして、地上をもっと自由度・開放性の高いものにしたいと思い、そのために雛壇造成を止め、いわゆるスロープ造成としました。そのため建物自体が土留めになるように計画して、下階はコンクリートにしているわけです。

Common City Hoshida 79

配置図 / Situation / 1:2000

In this project, 112 houses similar to House F and an assembly hall are spread all over the site. The most important point is that the project was developed as a slope. The site has an inclination of 10% and usually residential areas on such sloping terrain are transformed into terraces in Japan. It was my intention to create a place with a high degree of freedom and openness by scattering houses over the continuously expanding ground. For this reason I have kept the slope instead of creating a terraced site. As the building itself needed to function as a stopper against landslides, we planned the base of the house in concrete.

コモンシティ星田

北傾斜面の敷地全体にばらまかれた各住戸群の間に道路、緑道、水路が配置され、敷地全体が土木、建築というヒエラルキーが排され、住宅地全体が滑らかに連続し、住戸、街、地域環境、そして都市へ連続した世界となることが求められました。

Streets, greenways and waterways run between the houses that are scattered over the entire north sloping site and remove the hierarchy between architecture and infrastructure. It was a request to create a fluent continuity throughout the entire residential area and to establish a world that is continuous with the house, district, closer environment and the city.

雛壇造成というのはこれがぼくの土地だ、私の所有だ、ということをはっきりイメージさせるような空間をつくるわけです。それを相対化したいというようなことだったのです。この計画ではどこまでが道路でどこまでが住戸か分かりにくくなっています。住戸から街まで連続する、そして街全体に開いていく空間にしたいということであって、まさに自由度の高い街を創りたかったわけです。1992年に全体が完成しています。

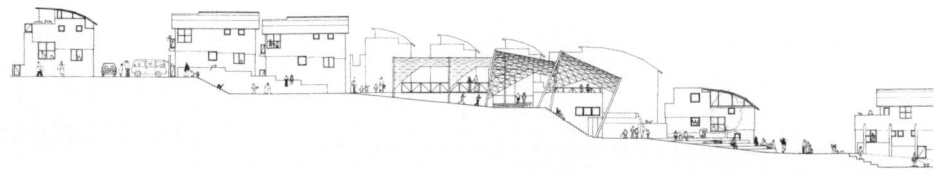

集会室前通路まわり + 中央緑道まわり立面図 / Elevation: Pathway, assembly hall + Greenway / 1:800

The terraced development creates a space that evokes a clear image in us: It is my land, it is my property. So I wished to relativise this image. In this design it is difficult to distinguish the border between the house and street. I wanted to create a space that continues from the house to the district and further opens up to the entire city and effectively builds a city with a high degree of freedom. The whole work was accomplished in 1992.

1994年に全体が竣工した公営の賃貸住宅です。長谷川逸子、松永安光両氏の設計と既存部の4者による混成でできています。各住棟は平行配置を避け、また逆に完全な囲い込みを避けることで曖昧な囲い込みによる開放的場所としての空間を確保しています。

Kumamoto Takuma Housing

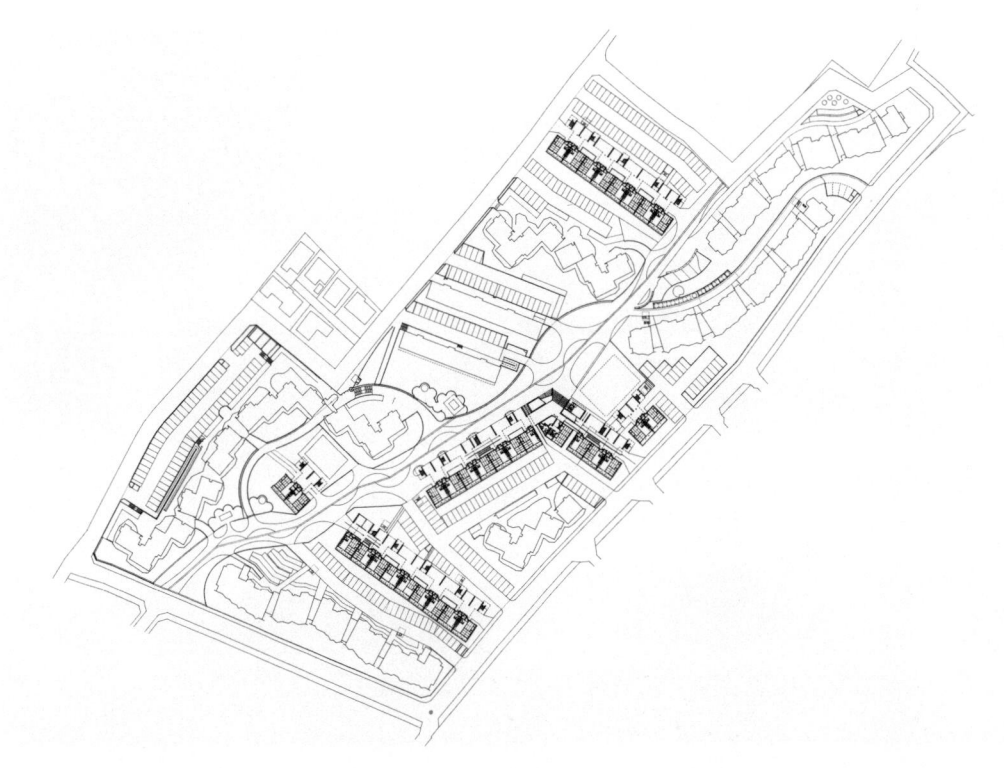

配置図 / Situation / 1:3000

This is a public apartment building for rental and the whole complex was constructed in 1994. It is a collective work including buildings by Itsuko Hasegawa, Yasumitsu Matsunaga and several existing buildings. The arrangement of each building avoids parallel placement as well as complete enclosure. By creating a space with an ambiguous enclosure, a place with open character is secured.

中央緑道から外部環境に続く外周道路に結ばれる各住棟の共有通路は敷地の傾斜面に沿いながらスロープ化して住棟内の各住戸を直接結びつけています。このことは、コモンスペースを排除したパブリックスペースでこの住宅地全体ができていることを意味します。

The public passage through each apartment building follows the topography as a slope and connects the central greenway with the outer ring street leading to the surrounding environment. At the same time, it also creates a direct access to each apartment. This means that the common space is removed and the whole residential site is entirely made of public space.

幕張ベイタウン・パティオス4番街

1995年に竣工した松永安光氏と共同設計による分譲の集合住宅です。この建物では四周の街路に沿って建つ4住棟に囲まれた2階の屋上である中庭が統合する構成となっています。この中庭は各住棟に穿たれて貫通する外部空間を伴い、重合関係をなすことで街まで連続する空間となっています。

This is a condominium apartment block in collaboration with Yasumitsu Matsunaga in 1995. In this composition, four apartment buildings are placed along the streets and the enclosed courtyard on the roof level above the first floor unites the whole. Since the courtyard includes the exterior public space, which penetrates through the apartment buildings, the courtyard implies an overlapping relationship and a space that is continuous within the city.

屋上庭園下部の地上階は各種店舗、駐車場が街路と中庭に引き込まれたパブリックな小広場に面して配置されています。このことで囲まれた中庭部もパブリックな空間となり、四辺の各住棟は内外両面でパブリック空間に面していることになります。このように、この集合住宅はコモンへの囲い込みとパブリックへの開放という矛盾する葛藤を内在する空間構成となっています。

Housing in Makuhari Baytown

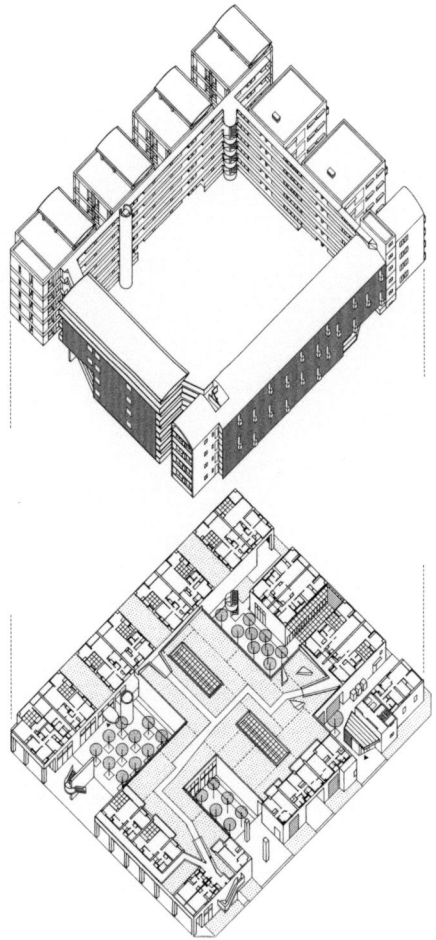

アクソノメトリック / Axonometry

Various shops and parking spaces are placed on the ground floor beneath the roof garden along the street and the small public square that is drawn into the courtyard. Accordingly, the enclosed courtyard becomes public and the four apartment buildings face both inside and outside the public space. Since the apartment buildings combine the enclosure of the common space as well as the opening towards the public space, the spatial composition implies a contradictory conflict.

建築の解放

The release of architecture

これは1999年に竣工した住宅です。雛壇造成された傾斜地に建っていた住宅の建て替えです。傾斜地に沿う道路に対応して分節されたスパイラル状に続く床の連続を敷地形状に沿って壁が囲み、屋根である覆いによって内部空間が形成されています。この大きな屋根は木造で、トラスも組まず板状の構成だけでつくっています。この屋根は太陽光を受ける集熱面が南向ということで決定されております。また床面は傾斜した地形に沿い、外周壁は敷地形状に沿って建てられており、このような外在的要因によって、この建物の全体は構成されています。

House SA   97

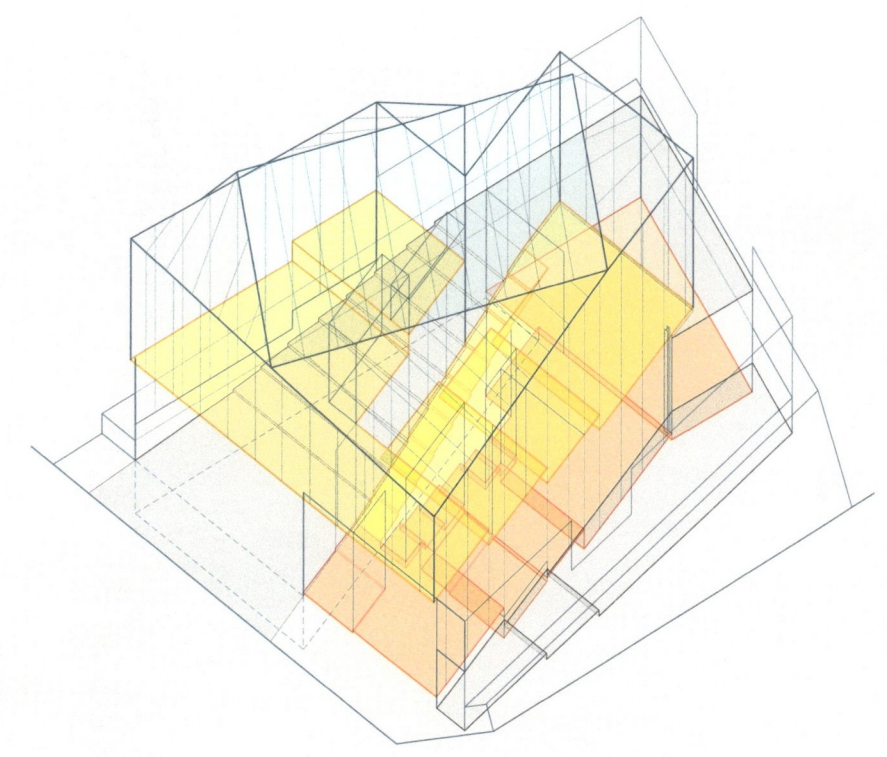

アクソノメトリック / Axonometry

This house was completed in 1999. It is a replacement of a former residence built on a terraced development of a sloping site. The segmented floors in the form of a continuous spiral follow the sloping street and are surrounded by walls along the boundary of the site. A big wooden roof made of a plate structure without any truss completes the interior space as a cover. The roof shape is defined by solar panels that are oriented towards the south. Since the floors follow the inclined topography and the exterior walls are placed along the site perimeter, the composition of the whole building is based on external factors.

言い替えれば、この建物は螺旋状の平面構成の形式の骨格を外在した要因によって決定された外皮によって包含されたものです。一般にこうした構成形式は建築のオブジェ的な魅力を形成するため、往々としてその形式自身を表現しがちになります。その結果、形態や構成の形式自体の表現主義的建築に陥る結果、その建物は彫塑的なものとなります。建築の形式はそこに展開する生活や活動の座標であるべきであり、それを構成するものが対象物として意味が形成されることを回避する必要があります。

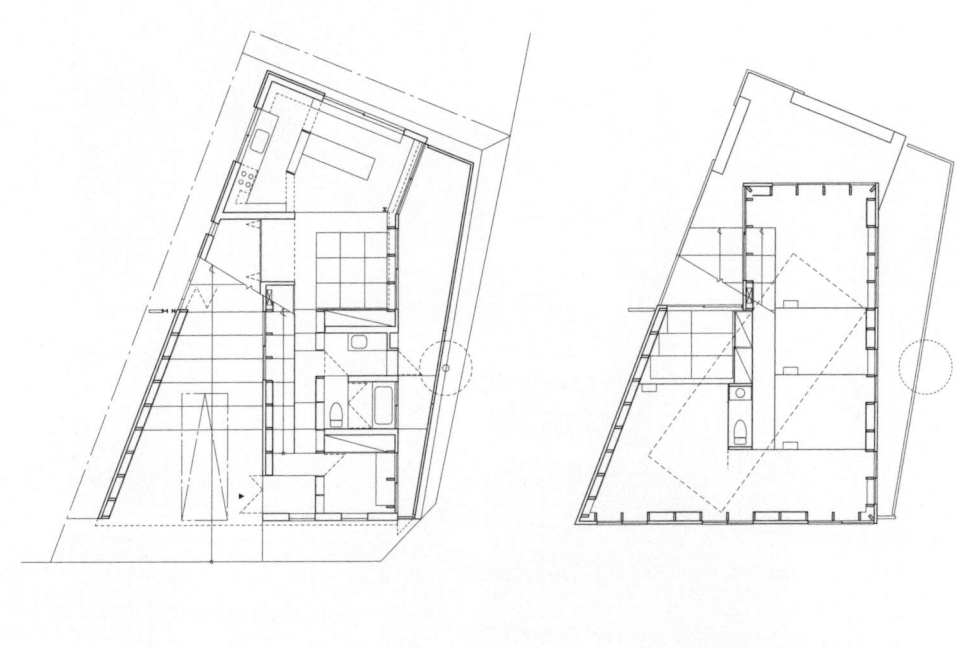

下階 + 上階平面図 / Lower floor + Upper floor / 1:250

In other words, the framework of the spiral composition in plan is placed within the outer layer that is defined by external factors. The compositional form as a spiral is usually expressed as a form itself to convey the appeal of the architectural object. The representation of form or composition leads to an expressionistic architecture and ultimately the building becomes sculptural. The architectural form should rather provide the base and reference for the emerging life and activity and it is necessary for the means of composition to avoid the meaning as an object.

この建物は、構成部位が外在的条件にそれぞれ独立して対応することによって形成されることから、部位が並列・併存して階層化・統合化せず断片化して非完結化していると言えます。またこの建物では、壁、天井等の多くの構成材は仕上げを施すことなく未仕上げ状態で仕上げております。さらに作り付け棚をはじめ多くの家具は使い古された古いものを使用しており、様々な時間を配列した状況が形成されています。これらのことはまさに時間的に重層化された日常性のうえにこの建物ができていることを示していると言えます。

In this building the composing elements respond independently to the external factors and coexist side by side without hierarchy and unification, establishing a fragmentation and incompleteness. Furthermore the walls, ceiling and many other components are carried out without any treatment and are left in an unfinished state. Also the built-in shelves and furniture are old and used, creating a state of various times placed next to each other. Considering these facts, we may say the building is based on the ordinariness as an accumulation of time.

2001年に竣工した小さく単純で開放的な別荘です。それほど広くない主室の天井の高さが3.6mです。また低い所は2.1m、そして1.7mとなっており、住宅としては、幾分スケールが普通と違うことから不思議な感覚を持たれると思います。そういうスケール的操作がある種の意味の宙吊り感を形成します。透視性、透光性のある嵌め殺しガラス、またスライドガラス戸を多用していることで透明性の高い空間となっています。

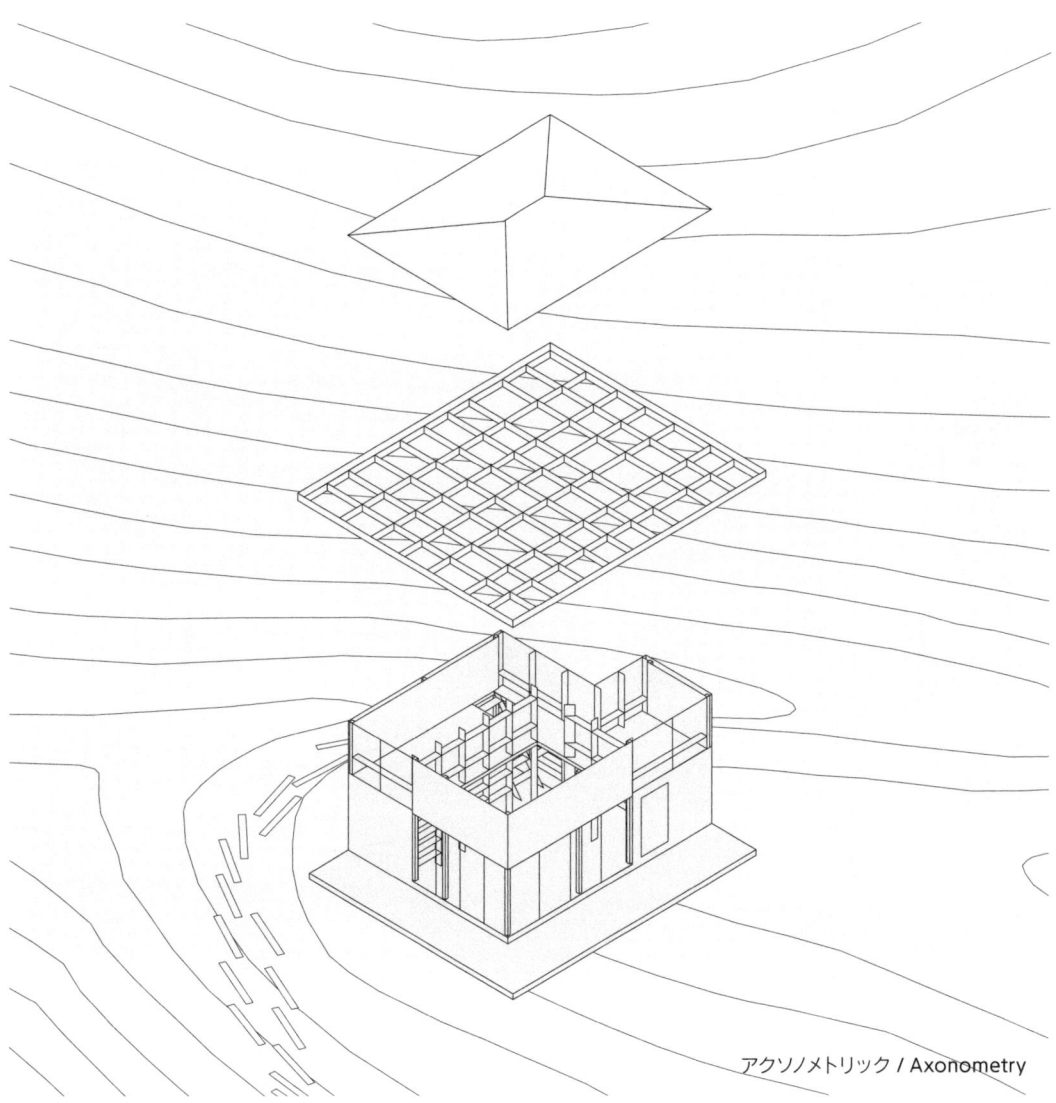

アクソノメトリック / Axonometry

This is a small, simple and open cottage completed in 2001. While the main room is not particularly big with a 3.6 m high ceiling, the lower spaces are 2.1 m and 1.7 m high. You may have a strange feeling, as the scale is rather different from a usual residence. Such operation on scale leads to a certain suspension of meaning. The frequent use of transparent and translucent fixed glazing and sliding doors establishes a highly transparent space.

建物各部が重合しあい、相互貫入し連続する空間となっており、こうした構成により外部の自然環境から連続し吹き抜け、通り抜けられる開放的な場としています。また覆い性の弱い軒庇に連続する平坦面の屋根、格子状スケルトンにまつわりつく断片化した建具の面などの構成材で、拡散性と浮遊感ある建物になっており、それらによって自由度の大きい開放性と解放性を形成していると考えています。

In this space, each part of the building is overlapping, interpenetrating and continuous. This composition creates a place with an open character, where the surrounding natural environment can continuously permeate and breeze through. Furthermore, components such as the flat roof continuing to the canopy with less sense of cover, and the fragmented surfaces of doors and furniture attached on the lattice skeleton, compose a building with a diffused and floating feeling. As a result, I think the building features an openness and release with a high degree of freedom.

2005年に竣工した「QUICO 神宮前」です。住宅と店舗、オフィスの複合建築です。建物の外形は、道路や隣地境界からの斜線制限等の法制度に対応した角錐状の塔状形態となっていますが、そのことを積極的に表現したり、その逆にその形を完璧に避けることを意図していません。その根拠を曖昧にしたまま形態化しています。一方、この内部はこのアクソメ断面図で見られるようにスキップフロアの連続で構成されています。

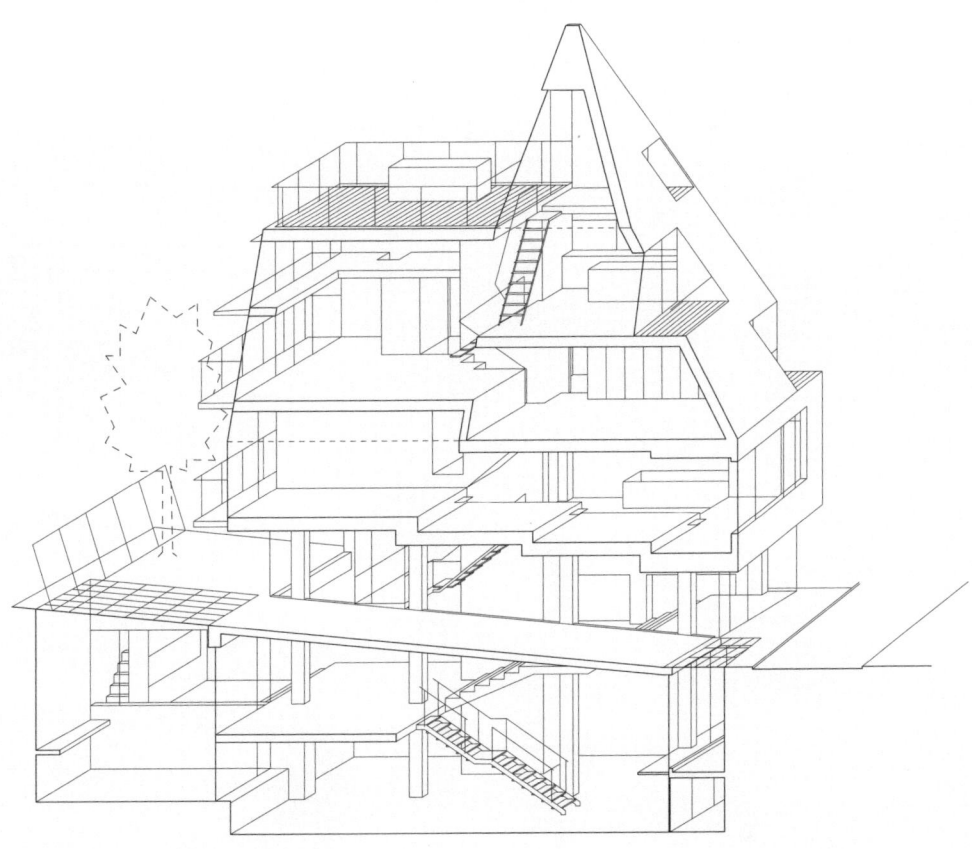

アクソノメトリック / Axonometry

This is QUICO Jingumae, completed in 2005. The building complex contains a shop, an office and a residence. The pyramid tower shape of the building arises from building law, which prescribes a diagonal height limitation along the parcel boundary and the street. I neither used this shape actively as expression, nor avoided it completely, thus the intention of finding the shape is left in ambiguity. As shown in the axonometric section, the interior space has a composition of continuous, skipping floors.

この建物は地階に店舗を設けています。そのことから周辺地域から地下へのスムーズなアクセスを可能とする連続性を必要としました。それゆえこの建物の地下は地上部と変わらぬ周辺の近接性を伴いながら、都市からの奥行きを伴ったものとなっています。この地階の店舗はスキップしながら段上の場を2層分繰り返した空間となっています。このことから、いわゆる地下都市の趣を呈する場となっています。

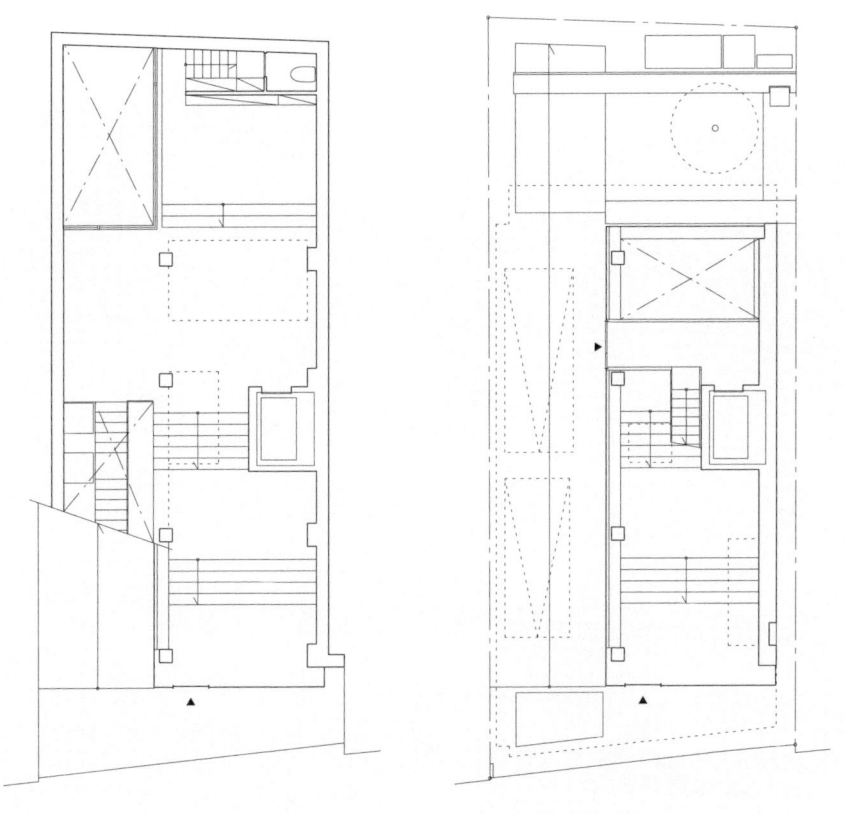

地下1階 + 1階平面図 / Basement floor + Ground floor / 1:200

In this building the shop is located in the basement. In order to enable smooth access, continuity between the surrounding environment and the basement was required. The basement of this building therefore contains a proximity to the surrounding environment as the above ground levels and yet an inner depth towards the city. The underground shop space is conceived as stepped places that skip continuously over two levels. The place therefore features the charm and qualities of an underground city.

住宅部は動線的に店舗、オフィスを抜けて、建物上部にスキップして重ねられた構成の内に位置付けられています。このことで、都市に対する浮遊性と連続性という対立的な場所の性格を合わせ持った空間となっています。建物の全体の内部は、このように店舗、オフィス、住宅が多層に折り重ねられた構成によって、都市に繋がれ広げられ重ねられた空間となっています。この建物は都市を構成する「スモール・コンパクト・ユニット」となっていると言えます。

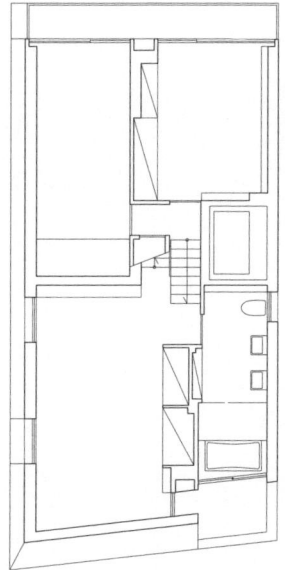
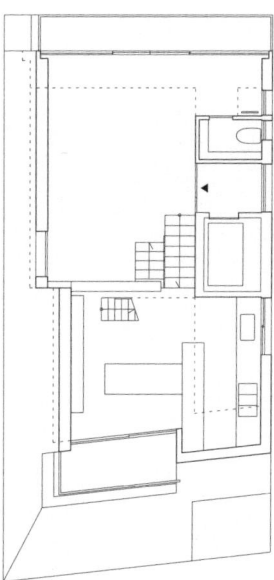

3階 + 4階平面図 / 2. + 3. floor / 1:200

The residential part is accessed by passing through the shop and office and is situated on the upper levels within the composition of skipping floors. Thus the space combines characteristics of contrasting places by including both the floating and continuous feeling towards the city. Through the folded and layered composition of the shop, office and residence, the whole interior space of the building is connected, extended and layered with the city. This building can be understood as a 'small compact unit' within the composition of the city.

スモール・コンパクト・ユニットとアイランド・プラン

Small compact unit and island plan

2004年と2013年に2棟竣工した建物で、東京の中心部から離れた西部地域の住宅地に大きなボリュームに纏めることなく分散した建物の集合で計画されました。交差メゾネット型を主とした5戸の住戸の立体的噛み合わせによる重層長屋形式の集合住宅です。このことは後で述べる「スモール・コンパクト・ユニットとアイランド・プラン」という考え方によるものです。

The two apartment buildings were completed in 2004 and 2013 in a western residential area outside the city centre of Tokyo. Instead of concentrating the project in a large volume, we planned it as group of scattered buildings. The apartment buildings comprise five dwelling units with mainly a crossing maisonette type that pile up spatially in a form of stacked row house. It is based on the concept of small compact unit and island plan that I will explain shortly.

この建物の外形は日本での見慣れた建物、特に集合住宅とはやや異なるスケールとプロポーションをもっています。わずかな違いですが、そのことが建物の類型的意味を曖昧にします。また外形各面がそれぞれ異なった仕上げによって、それぞれの面がこの建物のボリュームを形成しながら、かつ部分化し断片化するといった対立的な両義性をもたらしていると思います。

2階 + 3階平面図 / 1. + 2. floor / 1:200

The exterior form of this building has a rather different scale and proportion from common buildings and particularly apartment buildings in Japan. It is a small difference, but this makes the typological meaning of the building ambiguous. Furthermore, each side of the exterior form has a different finish. They compose the building volume, but as they include a fragmenting and separating character, a conflicting ambiguity is created.

この建物の構成により、各住戸は3方向および4方向の開口部をもち、それぞれ独立した外階段によって直接外部へのアクセスを可能としています。このことから各住戸は独立性の高い空間を獲得していると共に、都市や環境に対して連続的な空間になっています。

The composition of the building allows each residential unit to have openings towards three or four directions and enables direct access to the exterior with independent outside staircases. In this way each residential unit gains a space of high independency and yet one that is continuous with the city and the environment.

将来近似した2棟の建物が追加される予定となっています。そのことによる相乗効果によって今お話しした2つのことはより強調されるはずです。この計画のように建物全体をひとつのボリュームに纏めるのではなく、フットプリントを小さくしたボリュームに分離し、それを散在させる形式が都市環境にとって有効と考えました。この形式を「スモール・コンパクト・ユニットとアイランド・プラン」と呼びました。

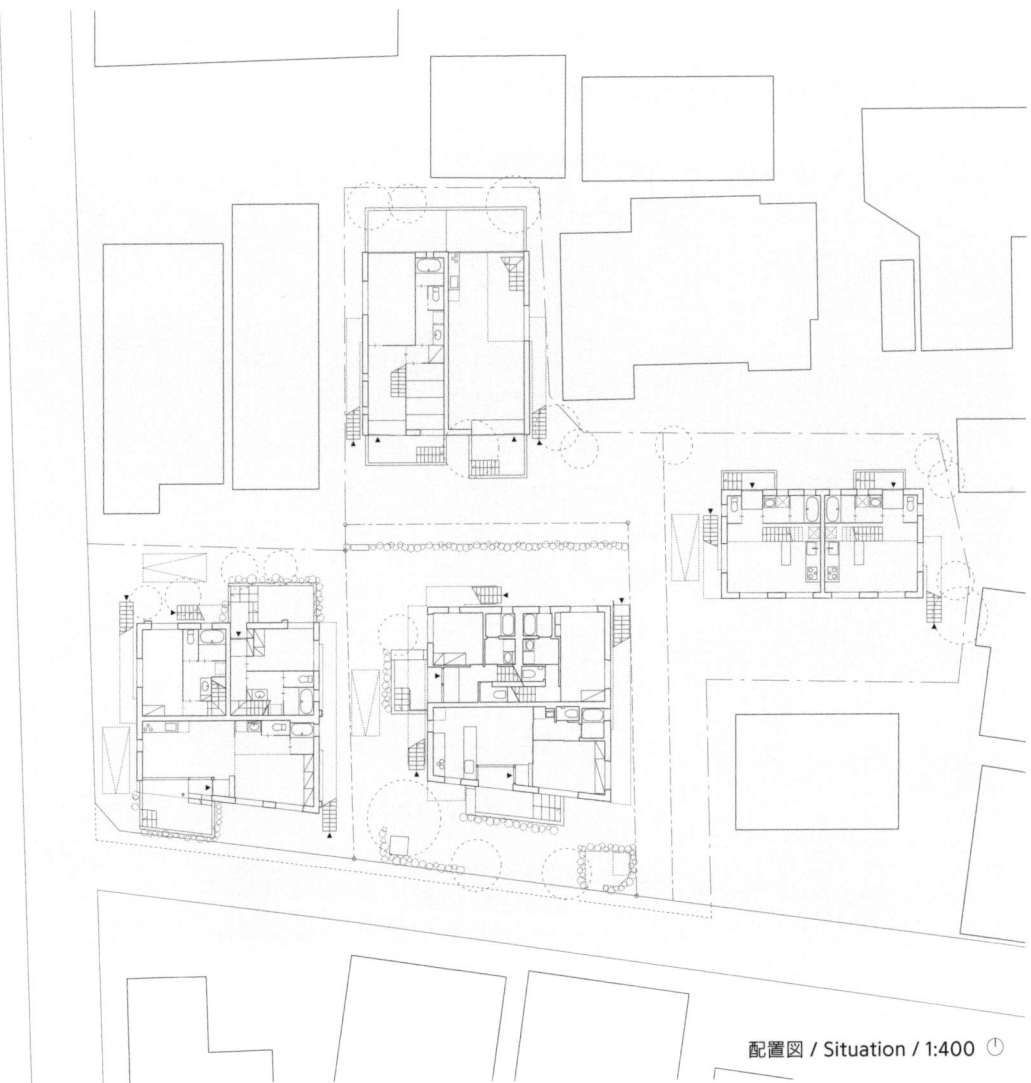

配置図 / Situation / 1:400

We are planning to add two more similar buildings in the near future. The two ideas mentioned before will surely be emphasized by the arising synergy effect. In this planning, the whole building is not concentrated in a single volume, but divided into several volumes with smaller footprints that are scattered over the site. I considered this compositional form to be effective for the urban environment and I called it 'small compact unit and island plan'.

ミュンヘンの「工作連盟ジードルング・ヴィーゼンフェルト」です。2006年4月にかけて行われたコンペの入選案です。約4haの土地に4階、8階、11階の3種の小さなフットプリントの41の住棟が島状に配されています。島状に配置された住棟から残ったランドスケープはそれぞれ住棟のプライバシーをまもりながら、均質的にその場所の広がりを連続させます。この計画は設計途中で政治的理由でストップしております。

Werkbundsiedlung Wiesenfeld

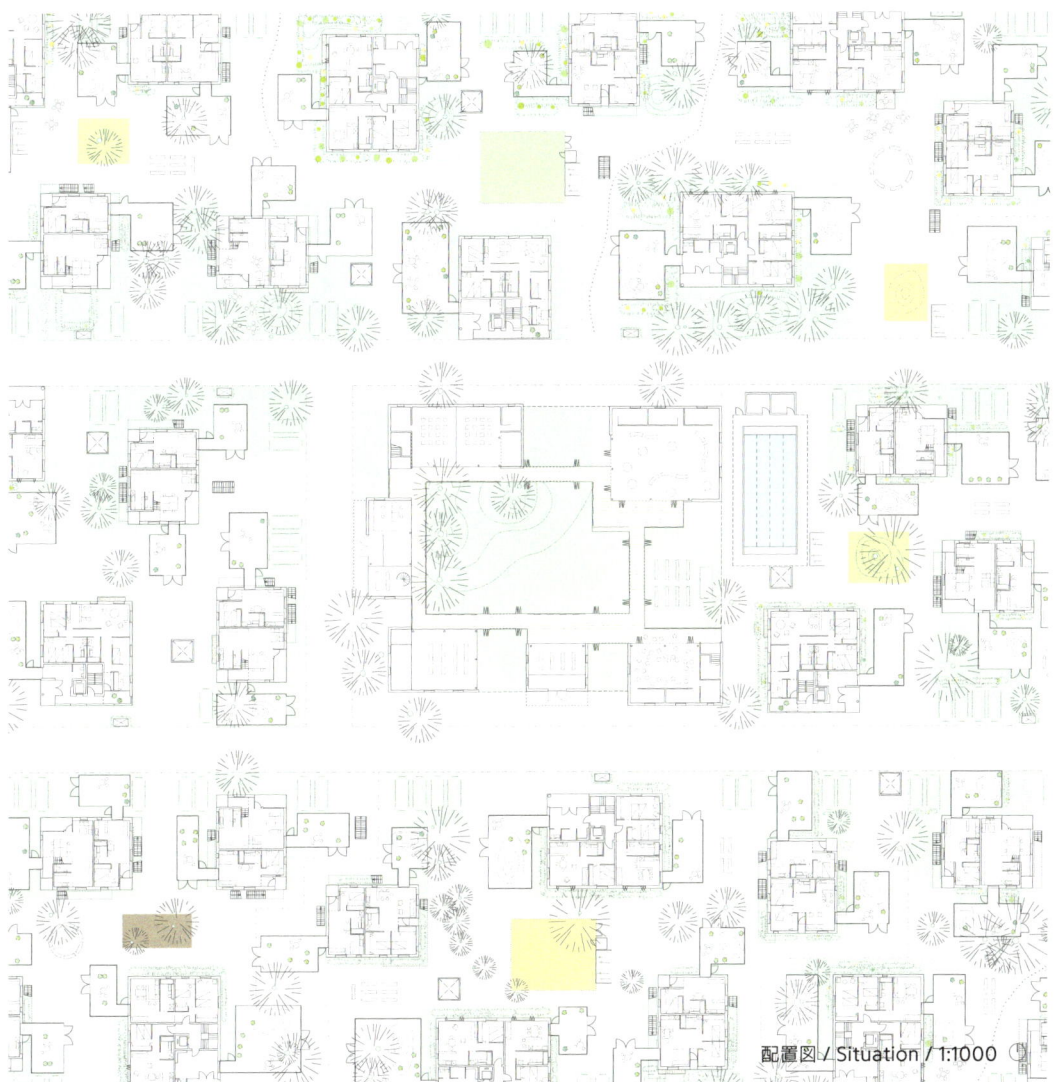

配置図 / Situation / 1:1000

This is the winning proposal for the competition Werkbundsiedlung Wiesenfeld in 2006 in Munich, Germany. Forty-one housing buildings of three types containing 4, 8 and 11 floors with small footprints are arranged like islands on the four-hectare site. The remaining landscape between the buildings provides privacy to each building and evenly creates a continuous expansion of the place. The project was stopped during the design phase for political reasons.

130　工作連盟ジードルング・ヴィーゼンフェルト

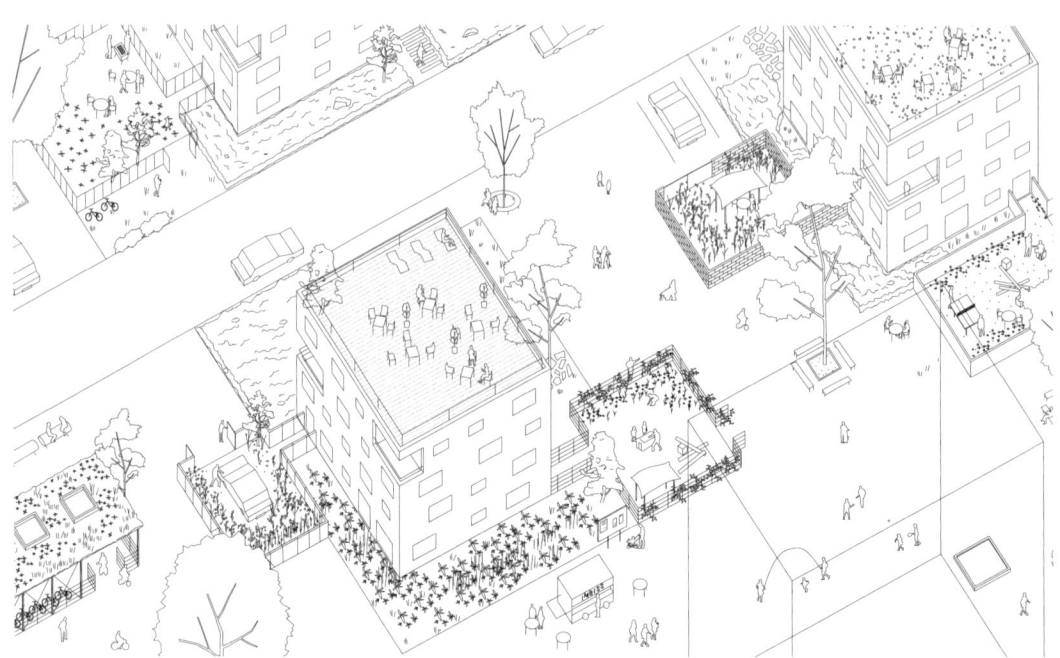

大地に連続的な低層部、高木の緑に共生する中層部、空や遠くを眺望できる高層部の3種の場所に対応した居住環境が形成されます。こうした建物の配置法によって、柔らかで瑞々しい新しい都市居住と環境が生まれるはずです。このプロジェクトにおいて、現実の条件のなかでいかにスモール・コンパクト・ユニットとアイランド・プランを求めようとしてきたかを理解していただければと思います。このことで開放的な内外を実現し、都市居住と都市環境の可能性を追求してきたと言えます。

The living environments are formulated according to the three kinds of places; the lower floors are continuous with the ground, the mid-floors are continuous with the trees and the upper floors have a distant view towards the sky. By arranging the buildings this way, surely a soft and refreshing environment for urban living will be created. You may understand how I strived for the small compact unit and island plan within the real conditions in this project. By doing so, I could realise spaces with an open character both inside and outside, and seek the possibilities and potential in urban living and the city environment.

開催候補都市であったミュンヘンでの2018年の冬期オリンピック村コンペティションの入選案です。その後開催地が韓国に決まり、この計画は実現されないこととなりました。予定では、オリンピック終了後はミュンヘンの大規模な集合住宅団地として使われる予定でした。Egota Houseや工作連盟ジードルング・ヴィーゼンフェルトと同様にスモール・コンパクト・ユニットとアイランド・プランの考え方でつくられた計画です。

Munich 2018 Winter Olympic Village

配置図 / Situation

This is an award winning proposal for the Olympic Village competition in Munich, then a candidate for the 2018 Winter Olympics. The Olympic Games were later awarded to South Korea and this project couldn't be implemented. It was planned to use it as a large-scale residential complex after the Olympic Games. Like the Egota House and the Werkbundsiedlung Wiesenfeld, the project is based on the concept of a small compact unit and island plan.

現実条件との葛藤による構成形式

Composition in tension with the reality

東京工業大学のキャンパス正門の脇に建つホールや会議室、レストラン等を含んだ駅前のコンプレックスです。この建物は大学構内にありながら、鉄道駅、広場、商店街、住宅地と様々な場所に囲まれています。また隣接して篠原一男設計の東工大百年記念館があります。百年記念館がオブジェ的な存在であるのに対し、この建物はより場所的、空間的構成の建物となっています。

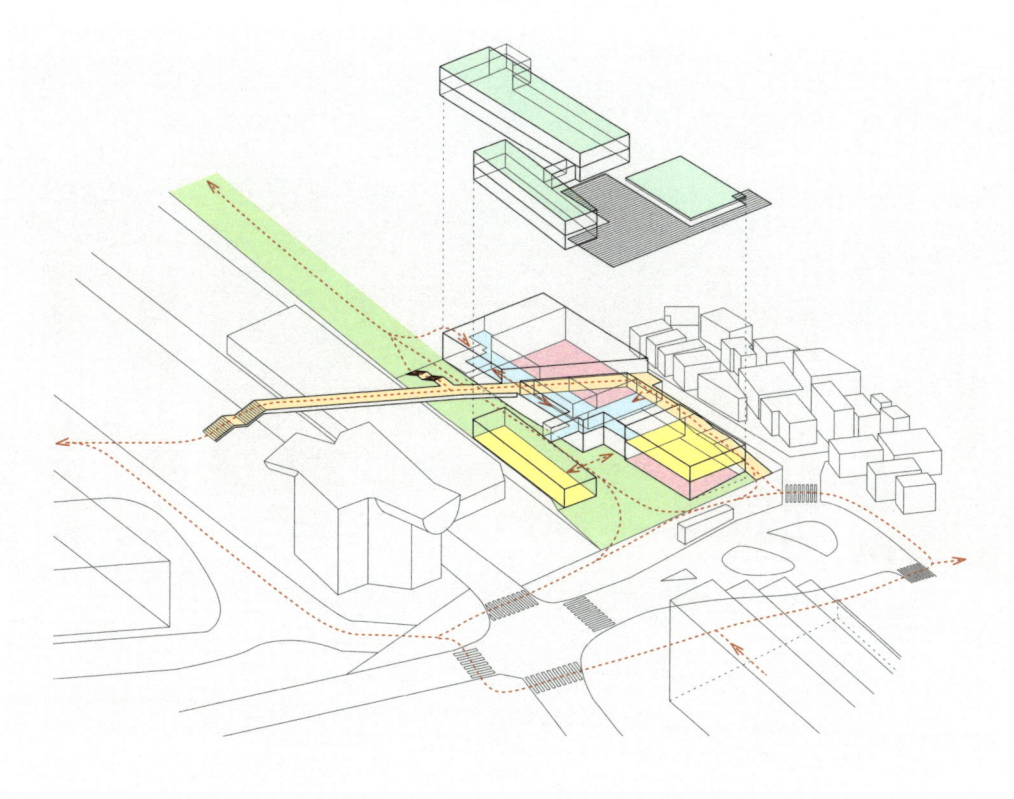

アクソノメトリック / Axonometry

This building complex contains halls, office spaces and restaurants. It faces the train station and is situated beside the main entrance to the campus of the Tokyo Institute of Technology. Although the building is located inside the university campus, it is surrounded by various places such as the plaza, train station, shopping street and residential area. Furthermore, the Centennial Hall by Kazuo Shinohara lies nearby. While the Centennial Hall has the expression of an object, this building is rather conceived as a composition of places.

この建物は高さを抑え、機能毎に建物ボリュームを分節、分散して、それらをルーバー状の庇が繋げ、全体を統合しています。庇は鉄道の駅前広場に大きく張り出し、都市と建物を連結する役割も担っています。ガラスと押し出し成形セメント板のニュートラルな外観は、こうした周囲の都市環境への対応であるとともに隣接する百年記念館へのリスペクトでもあります。

The height of the building is kept low and the building volume is divided and separated in each function, whereby the eaves connect and unite them to a whole. The eaves are strongly projected towards the station plaza and take over the role of connecting the building and the city. The neutral external appearance of glass and cement paneling corresponds to the surrounding city environment, but is also a sign of respect towards the adjacent Centennial Hall.

駅前広場に面した屋外アトリウムはこの建物の各部への接続点であると同時に広場であり、ゲートであり、コネクションとなって大学の様々な場所へ自由に繋げ、アクセスできる場所となっています。今お話したこの建物に関わる周辺環境や様々な使用用途によるコンプレックスはこの建物が成立する現実的条件と言えます。この条件は、現代社会や今日の環境での様々な対立や矛盾を内包しています。こうした対立を調整し、矛盾を包含する建築の構成形式が現代建築の可能性を示す、と考えるようになりました。

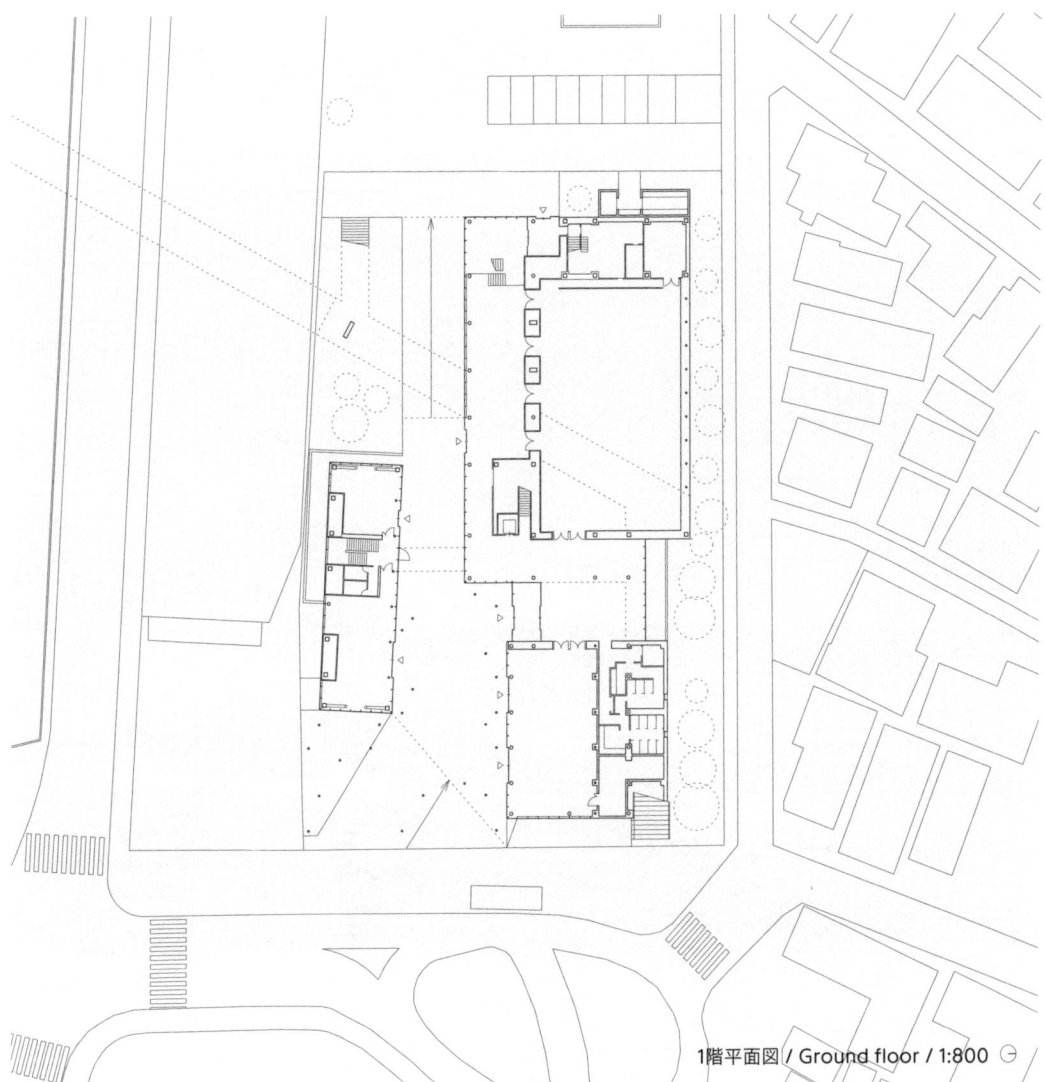

1階平面図 / Ground floor / 1:800

The exterior atrium facing the station plaza is an access point to the different building parts, but as it is also a plaza and a gate, it is a place of connection that enables free access and a link to the various locations of the university. The varying surrounding environments and different functions I have mentioned before are the conditions of reality that give existence to the building. These conditions include the conflicts and contradictions deriving from the present society and environment. I come to think that the compositional form, which balances conflicts and includes contradictions, reveals the possibilities and potential of contemporary architecture.

宇土市立網津小学校

この小学校は低層で、複数のヴォールト屋根の集合で構成され、平面的に広がる内外の空間となっています。この小さな小学校は九州熊本県の海辺に近い農家が散在する田園地帯のなかに近い山並みに呼応するなど、その風景に連続するように建っています。3列の教室が廊下を介して一体化しており、動線や視線が多方向に抜けて児童の様々な活動が自在に展開する場となっています。

Amitsu Primary School

1階平面図 / Ground floor / 1:800

This low-rise elementary school in Amitsu is composed as an assembly of multiple vaulted roofs with horizontally expanding internal and external spaces. This small elementary school in the Kumamoto Prefecture lies in a rural area in between dispersed farmhouses near the sea. Like the roof standing in dialogue with the surrounding mountain range, the building is intended to be continuous with the landscape. Three rows of classrooms with corridors in between are united and enable views and movements to expand in different directions, creating a place where various activities can develop freely.

146　宇土市立網津小学校

一部2層の平屋建てのこの建物はより水平に広がった空間になっており、同時に田園地帯の外部に連続してこの広がりが展開するよう形成されています。軒高を抑えた2種類のライズをもつヴォールト状の屋根は連続して架けられることで、均質な架構の中に多くの空間的纏まりをつくっています。左の写真は1階の低学年用の教室、右の写真は2階の上級生のための教室です。それぞれ大きなヴォールトと対応しています。

Amitsu Primary School

The space of this partly two-storey building spreads out in the plane and is conceived to develop continuously towards the exterior rural landscape. The roof with two differently rising vaults is kept low and its repetition creates many spatial entities within the homogenous structure. The classroom of the lower grades is presented in the left image and the classroom of the higher grades in the right image. The size of the classrooms and the big vaults correspond to each other.

この屋根の組み合わせによって妻面側に生じる「ずれ」がハイサイドライトとなり、3列の教室等に様々な光や換気・通風をもたらし、奥深い内側にも明るい爽やかな場所を与えています。この「ずれ」は不合理を内在化した合理の構成を意味します。なお、左の写真は手前の教室から左奥に音楽室、右奥に理科室が見えて、それぞれの連続した関係がわかります。なお、右の写真は中央列の図書室。この部分に2階がのっています。

The combination of the two different vaults creates a gap on the gable side that becomes a high-sided light. It provides the three rows of classrooms with various light and ventilation and creates a bright and refreshing place in the deepest internal spaces. This gap means an irrationality that is inherent in the rational composition. In the left image of the classroom, we can recognise the music room on the left and the science room on the right, and understand the continuous relationship between them. The image on the right shows the library in the middle row, upon which the upper floor is situated.

閉じた箱の開放

Opening of the closed box

「水無瀬の町家」北側に中庭を介して2008年に増築したものです。38年後に増築されたことで、この両者の建物の考え方の違いが現れています。隣接する周囲の既存建物との関係から配置されていますが、特に主屋である「水無瀬の町家」との間隔が近くもなく遠くでもない距離に位置付き、断面や配置の扱いによって曖昧な関係のまま、残った空地を中庭として、全体が弱い統合性によって纏められています。

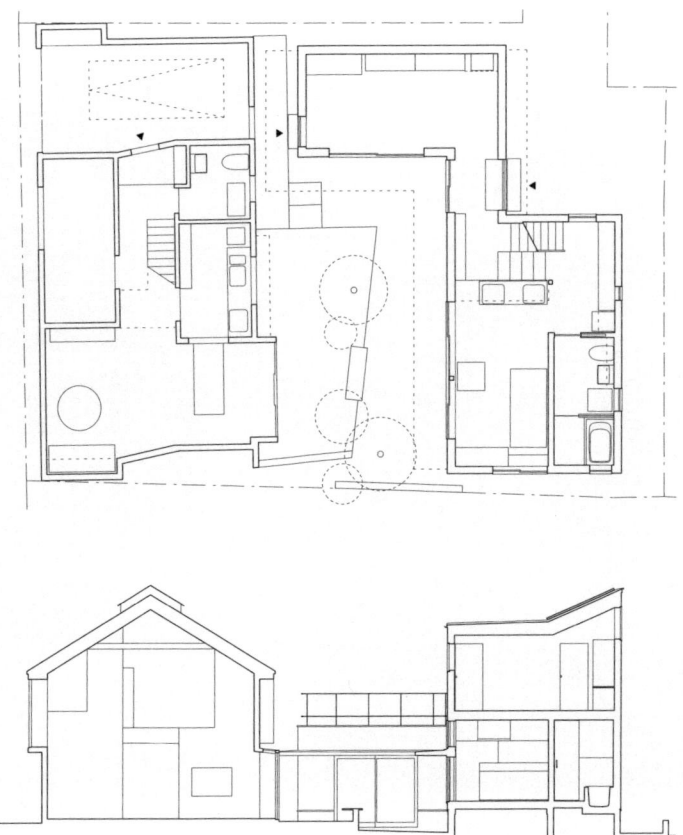

1階平面図 + 断面図 / Ground floor + Section / 1:200

This is an extension of the Townhouse in Minase in 2008 across the inner garden on the north side. Because it is an extension after 38 years, the difference in the way of thinking about these two buildings is visible. Although the extension is placed in relation to the neighbouring buildings, the whole is ordered through a weak unification. Especially the distance between the main building and the extension is neither close nor far. Furthermore the treatment of the section and the placement of the buildings create an ambivalent relationship, whereby the remaining open space becomes an inner garden.

「水無瀬の町家」の主室の中心性をもった天井の高いクライマックス的空間とは対照的に、この建物では、中庭に沿って天井の低いいくつかの室が連続して配置されており、ノンヒエラルキカルな空間構成となっています。特に両者の空間構成と造られた時の違いを、両建物が面する中庭によって調整されています。

In contrast to the main space of the Townhouse in Minase, with its centrality and high ceiling as climax space, the extension building is based on the non-hierarchical space composition as a series of low rooms along the inner garden. Especially the differences in composition of space and time of construction are adjusted by the inner garden where both buildings face each other.

この「散田の家」は、その後建てられた別棟と一緒に2013年に改築されました。約45年後での改築によって、当時と現在との空間に関しての考え方の違いが分かります。「散田の家」では、「閉じた箱」という私の当時の空間概念による閉鎖的空間を構成しましたが、この「改築 散田の家」は、主屋のイメージの変更と別棟との再統合により「閉じた箱」という概念的空間が開くことになったと思っております。主屋と別棟がつくられた時代に対応して空間観が異なっていることによる違いと同時に、両者に相補関係がもたらされたことによって、空間の対立関係が鮮やかになったと考えます。

House in Sanda Renovation   157

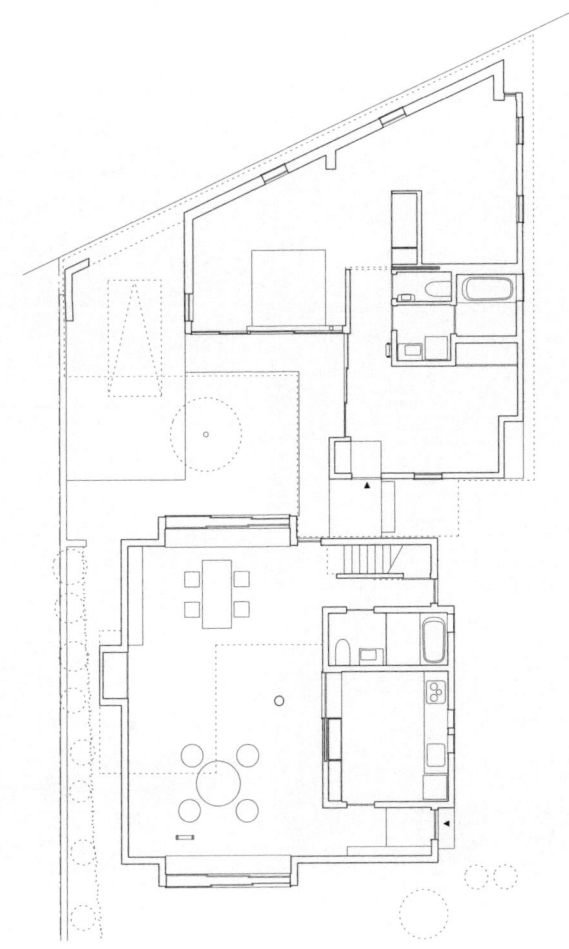

1階平面図 / Ground floor / 1:200

This House in Sanda and the later extension were renovated together in 2013. Through this renovation after 45 years, the difference in the way of thinking about space at that time and today can be understood. For the House in Sanda, I composed a space with a closed character based on my concept of space at that time, called the closed box. For the House in Sanda Renovation, by modifying the image of the main house and recreating a unity together with the extension, I think the concept of space called closed box could be opened. The main house and the extension have a different conception of space due to the different construction period. By creating a complementary relationship, the contrast between these two spaces could become more vivid and clear.

この改築に際し、「散田の家」の構成全体の骨格を残しながら、新たなイメージの空間を求められました。そのことから、建物自体の構成の変更は最小限にとどめ、主屋の内部空間全体のイメージを支配していた内壁、天井そして柱等の生地仕上げの木材を薄い白色系ペイントで仕上げることで、素材感を曖昧に残しながらの空間のイメージの変更を行いました。また、別棟の減築や中庭の再構成によって、有機的な全体の再統合を意図しました。この改築によってヴィラから都市住宅である町家へ改変したことと同時に「閉じた箱」の開き方を示したものであったと考えます。

A new image of the space was required for the renovation, while preserving the framework of the overall composition of the House in Sanda. For that, modifications in the composition of the building itself were kept to a minimum. The inner walls, ceiling and the column in natural wood, which controlled the image of the interior space, were painted thinly in whitish colour. In this way, the interior space of the main house could be modified, while preserving the materiality in an ambiguous way. Also by reducing the volume of the extension building and by rearranging the inner garden, I intended to unify the whole in an organic way. Through this renovation, the villa could be transformed into a townhouse and at the same time the opening of the closed box could be revealed.

オーディナリーな解放的空間

The liberated ordinary space

今日の掌握できぬ複雑な社会状況、不安定で矛盾に満ちた世界に拘束された精神や身体に対していかにこうした社会や世界に共存させうる自由な空間を成立させるかが私の最大のテーマであったとでも言えましょうか。それは、私達を枠付けている様々な環境、例えば文化環境、そして特に建築によって拘束された空間を解放し、それから自由であり得る空間と言えます。つまりきめつけず、とらわれない心身の自由さの確保のなかで愉しく、豊かで、柔らかに住め、生きることを可能とさせる空間です。つまり可能性を求めた空間です。

こうした空間は、一見なにげなく、どこにもありそうですが、しかしどこにもない空間のように思われます。それは、私達が生活してきた空間を隔絶したものでなく、歴史的に文化的に連続したものの中に自由度を与える空間であります。つまり時間的、空間的に現実世界と連続することで、完結したものでなく、未完的で非完結な世界です。

My biggest theme lies in my search for the free space that can enable the spirit and body to coexist with the restricting society of today, which is uncontrollable and complex, full of uncertainty and contradiction. This means liberating the space from various restricting environments such as the cultural environment and especially from the restraint of architecture, in order to create a space that can be free. By ensuring a free mind and body without constraint and fixation, the space creates the possibility of a soft, joyful and rich habitation and life. This is namely a space that seeks possibility.

Such space seems to exist everywhere at first sight, however I feel that this space exists nowhere. This space is not detached from our daily space in life and ensures a possible degree of freedom within the continuity of culture and history. By being connected to the real world in time and space, it is not a completed, but an unfinished and incomplete space.

こうした日常的空間と連続する空間とは、例えば、「ありそうでない空間」のように、現実に似ていて、しかしそれではない空間と言えます。ですから「Aでありながら非Aである空間」また「AでありながらBである空間」といった現実の世界に準拠して意味的に相反的、矛盾的、両義的、そしてまた対立的、複眼的関係を含んだ空間と言えそうです。こうした意味を包含した空間は、その空間に紋切り方に内在した意味を曖昧にし、それに関わる文脈の変更を求め、意味の宙吊り、消去とも言うべき、意味作用に揺さぶりをかけることになります。

私達の生活し、活動する空間の枠組みは一般的に文化的環境として類型化し、制度化しているわけですが、こうした意味の宙吊り、消去はその制度に揺さぶりをかけ、意味の固定化を避けるということで、そのような制度からの解放を促し、そこから自由な世界が現れると考えています。このことは、紋切り化した類型に対して様々な意味的な制度による拘束からの解放によって得られる自由だと言えます。

We can say that such spaces connected to ordinary space are similar but not identical to the real world, like spaces which seem to exist, but actually don't. These spaces can be described of being 'A but not A' or at the same time 'A and B'. They follow the real world, but contain a conflicting, contradicting and ambiguous meaning as well as the relationship of contrast and multiple viewpoints. Spaces with such character lead the inherent typical meaning of space to ambiguity, as well demand the modification of the related context. Furthermore, by means of suspension and erasure, they shake the significance and function of the meaning.

The framework of space in which we live and work is generally typified and institutionalised as our cultural environment. Through the suspending and erasing of meaning, which shake the institutionalised system and avoid the fixation of meaning, I believe it is possible to stimulate liberation from such a system, leading to a free world. Finally, I may say the freedom from typological fixation could be achieved through the release from the various restraints that are derived from the institutionalisation of meaning.

建築を考える自由

長谷川豪

坂本一成はメンドリジオでのレクチャーをこう切り出した。
「私の設計した建物は日本でも理解しがたい建築と言われますが、その理由の多くは私の建物に強い表現がない事に拠ると思います。」
曰く、建築が強いあるいは特異な形態をもたないし、ダイナミックでもヒロイックでもないし、クライマックスもないからだという。この出だしの発言は坂本の師にあたる篠原一男を代表とする「強い表現」に自分の表現を対比させたものであるが、この一文には坂本の建築観の2つの特徴が明確に表れているように思われる。

まずは「私の建物に強い表現がない」。

坂本は自作を語るとき、よく「〜ではないもの」という言い方をする。例えば「南湖の家」の7寸5分の勾配をもつ切妻屋根の断面について、それよりも屋根を急にするとだんだん厳しい<ゴシック>、緩くするとあたたかくやさしい<ロマネスク>だと感じ、また矩勾配は幾何学的な力をもつが、「それらのすべての空間は消えなければならなかった」とし、そうした歴史的に色づけられた意味に頼らないもの、「まさに意味が消えた、ただの断面という建築的言語であれば良いと考えるのだ」と述べている*。坂本は言葉に慎重な建築家である。言説ではアフォリズム的な表現は避けられ、なかなか「Aである」と断定せず、「Aでないもの」あるいは「AでありBでありCでもあるもの」などという。そこが坂本一成の真骨頂であり、両義性・多義性をもつ建築のリアリティについてはこのレクチャーの終盤でも語られた。両義性・多義性を求めるがゆえに、坂本の言説は必ずしも歯切れが良いわけではないのだが、しかし今回のレクチャーはいつもと少し趣が異なっていた。坂本の作品が必ずしも良く知られていない海外というコンテクストゆえに、そしてレクチャーという形式性ゆえに、さらには英語に同時通訳されるという状況ゆえに、これまでの言説と比べると単刀直入に建築思想が語られているように感じた。だからこそレクチャー後にスイスの若い建築家や学生から多くの反響があったのだろう。そうした単刀直入な坂本の言葉はこれまでの著作にはなかった、この本の一つの固有性だといえるだろう。

もう一つは「理解しがたい建築」。

いまは「理解しやすい建築」が受け入れられる時代だといえるかもしれない。情報技術の発達によって建築メディアが変容し、イメージが一瞬で世界中に届けられるようになった。明快で、分かりやすく、直ちに人々の共感

Freedom to think architecture
Go Hasegawa

Kazunari Sakamoto begins his lecture in Mendrisio with the following words: "My architecture is said to be difficult to understand in Japan. I think the biggest reason is there is no strong expression in my designs."
From his perspective, this is due to an architecture that doesn't have a unique form or climax, and is neither strong, dynamic nor heroic. These initial words on the expression of his own architecture are set in contrast to the "strong expression" represented by his teacher Kazuo Shinohara, yet they also reveal two characteristics of Sakamoto's architectural thinking.
Firstly: "There is no strong expression in my designs."
Sakamoto often applies the expression of denial to describe his own work. For instance, he illustrates the section of the gabled roof in the House in Nago with the inclination of 7.5 to 10 as follows: While a steeper roof gradually leads to the austere space of the Gothic, the warm and gentle space of the Romanesque gradually appears through the less inclined roof. Furthermore, the 1 to 1 inclination produces a geometrical strength. Sakamoto states that "all these spaces had to disappear" and without being dependent on those meanings coloured by history, he concludes that "this section is nothing else than the architectural language that has detached from any kind of meaning."* Sakamoto is an architect who chooses his words with care. His words avoid the expression of aphorism and he rarely calls things "A", but rather "not A" or even "A and B and C". This is the true value of Kazunari Sakamoto; in the lecture he also mentions the double meaning and ambiguity within the reality of architecture. As he seeks that double meaning and ambiguity, his words are not always clear. However, this lecture had a different expression. As the lecture took place abroad, where his works are not necessarily known, and due to the format of the lecture, which was translated simultaneously into English, his architectural ideas were presented directly and explicitly compared to his past statements. This surely is a reason for the great amount of interest and reactions of students

を得る建築が善とされ、少しでも分かりにくい議論は専門性のなかで閉じていて排他的だと糾弾される、そんな時代である。しかし坂本は、その長いキャリアのなかで、意識的に「理解しがたい」建築をつくってきたと言って良いだろう。学生のときに「なぜ代田の町家の中庭にベンチを設けたのですか？」と質問したことがある。坂本はこう答えた。「あそこにベンチがない状態をイメージするとその理由が分かるかもしれない」。はぐらかされているように聞こえるかもしれないが、安易に、一面的に建築を理解しないように注意された気がした。

じわじわと理解して、数年かけてなんとなく分かる、そういう建築を坂本は手がけてきたのではないか。それは建築を「直ちに理解する」ことの危うさ、そしてその不可能性を私たちに知らせているかのようである。「理解する」と人間はそれ以上考えを深めることを止めてしまうところがある。つまり坂本の「理解しがたい」建築は、別の言い方をすれば人々に時間をかけて能動的に考えることを求める建築であり、だから結果的に、他のどの建築家の仕事よりも実に多様な受け取られかたをしているように思われる。それは難解で閉じた議論に居直ることではないどころか、建築を考える意志と自由を、私たちに与えているのである。

* 「住宅における建築性」『坂本一成 住宅―日常の詩学』、TOTO出版、2001

and young architects after the lecture. This direct and explicit statement is a peculiarity of this publication, which cannot be found in the past writings of Sakamoto.

Secondly: "Architecture that is difficult to understand."
We may say that the current period welcomes architecture that is easy to understand. The development of information technology has transformed architecture media and an image can be sent within seconds all over the world. Clear and understandable architecture that evokes immediate sympathy is considered to be of value today, while hardly understandable discussions are accused of being exclusive and closed in their own field. Sakamoto however always followed the intention to create "architecture that is difficult to understand" throughout his career. I once asked him as a student: "Why did you place the bench in the courtyard of the Townhouse in Daita?" Sakamoto simply replied: "Imagine the house without the bench and you may discover the reason." His answer may seem evasive, but I understood it as a warning not to understand architecture easily and one-sidedly.

Sakamoto has apparently been creating architecture that we only understand gradually and somehow grasp after several years. It is as if he would point out the danger and impossibility of understanding architecture immediately. Once things are understood, people often stop deepening their thoughts. In other words, Sakamoto's "architecture that is hard to understand" can be described as an architecture that asks people to think actively and take their time. As a result, the architecture of Sakamoto seems to generate a perception and understanding that is more diverse than works of any other architects. It is not only far from being an abstruse and closed discussion, it even gives us the freedom and the will to think about architecture.

---

* "Architecturality in the dwelling", in: *Kazunari Sakamoto House: Poetics in the ordninary*, TOTO Publisher, Tokyo, 2001

出版支援者 / Supporters of this publication:

BSA Bund Schweizer Architekten

Medine Altiok, Julian Amann, Mario Beeli, Dan Budik, Francesco Buzzi, Mimosa Ceratti, Max Collomb, Julien Correia, Christian Dehli, Tom Dowdall, Wim Eckert, Koichi Endo, Lorenzo Fassi, Axel Gassmann, Daniel Giezendanner, Christian Gork, Malik Hammadi, Office Haratori, Daniel Hediger, Zerah Jentsch, Rodrigo Jorge, Masamichi Kawakami, Neven Kostic, Jonas Krieg, Sho Kurokawa, Alessandro Mattle, Christian Mueller Inderbitzin, David Orkand, Andréanne Pochon, Jonas Ryser, Juri Schönenberger, Jonas Staehelin, Mio Tachibana, Ilkay Tanrisever, Alexander Tochtermann, Koichiro Tsuchiya Sugiyama, Kana Ueda Thoma, Yushi Uehara, Julia Voormann, Laurent de Wurstemberger

坂本一成

略歴

1943	東京に生まれる
1966	東京工業大学建築学科卒業
1971	東京工業大学大学院博士課程を経て、武蔵野美術大学建築学科専任講師
1977	同助教授
1983	東京工業大学助教授
1991	同教授
2009	東京工業大学を定年退職、同名誉教授 現在、アトリエ・アンド・アイ 坂本一成研究室主宰

受賞

1990	日本建築学会賞作品賞「House F」
1992	村野藤吾賞「コモンシティ星田」
2013	日本建築学会著作賞『建築に内在する言葉』

書籍

1986	『現代建築 空間と方法10 坂本一成』同朋社出版
1994	『構成形式としての建築―コモンシティ星田を巡って』INAX出版
1996	『対話・建築の思考』共著：多木浩二、住まいの図書館出版局
1998	『ハウジング・プロジェクト・トウキョウ』共著：都市環境構成研究会、東海大出版会
2001	Maisons/Houses 1969-2001: Vers l'Espace Ouvert/Toward Open Space, Éditions du Moniteur, Paris 『坂本一成 住宅―日常の詩学』TOTO出版
2002	『建築を思考するディメンション―坂本一成との対話』共著、TOTO出版
2004	Kazunari Sakamoto Häuser/Houses, Edition Detail, Munich
2008	『坂本一成｜住宅』新建築社
2011	『建築に内在する言葉』TOTO出版 『建築的詩学 対話・坂本一成的思考』東南大学出版
2012	『空間構成学 建築デザインの方法』共著、実教出版
2013	『坂本一成 住宅めぐり』フリックスタジオ

Kazunari Sakamoto

Biography

1943	Born in Tokyo, Japan
1966	Graduated from the Architecture Department, Tokyo Institute of Technology
1971	After completing his doctorate at the Tokyo Institute of Technology, Lecturer at the Musashino Arts University
1977	Associate Professor at the Musashino Arts University
1983	Associate Professor at the Tokyo Institute of Technology
1991	Professor at the Tokyo Institute of Technology
2009	Professor Emeritus at the Tokyo Institute of Technology
	Established Atelier and I, Kazunari Sakamoto Architectural Laboratory

Awards

1990	Architectural Institute of Japan Award for House F
1992	Togo Murano Award for Common City Hoshida
2013	Architectural Institute of Japan Award for 'Language inherent in Architecture'

Bibliography

1986	Contemporary Architecture Space and Concept 10: Kazunari Sakamoto, Dohosha Publisher, Tokyo
1994	Architecture as a form of composition: Common City Hoshida, INAX Publisher, Tokyo
1996	Dialogue: Architectural thought, co-author with Koji Taki, Sumai no Toshokan Publisher, Tokyo
1998	Housing Project Tokyo, co-author, Tokai University Press, Kanagawa
2001	Maisons/Houses 1969–2001: Vers l'Espace Ouvert/Toward Open Space, Éditions du Moniteur, Paris
	Kazunari Sakamoto, House: Poetics in the Ordinary, TOTO Publisher, Tokyo
2002	Dimensions of Thinking on Architecture: Dialogue with Kazunari Sakamoto, TOTO Publisher, Tokyo
2004	Kazunari Sakamoto Häuser/Houses, Edition Detail, Munich
2008	Kazunari Sakamoto/Houses, Shinkenchiku-sha Publisher, Tokyo
2011	Language inherent in Architecture, TOTO Publisher, Tokyo
	Poetics in Architecture, Conversation: Kazunari Sakamoto, Southeast University Press, Nanjing
2012	Composition of Space: Method on Architectural Design, co-author, Jikkyou Publisher, Tokyo
2013	Introduction to Architect Kazunari Sakamoto's Works, Flick Studio, Tokyo

作品目録

1969	散田の家／東京都八王子市*
1970	水無瀬の町家／東京都八王子市*
1971	登戸の家／千葉県千葉市
1973	雲野流山の家／千葉県流山市*
	計画 K／神奈川県茅ヶ崎市
1974	計画 AN／神奈川県横浜市
	計画 N／長野県諏訪市
	計画 S／東京都世田谷区
1976	代田の町家／東京都世田谷区*
1978	南湖の家／神奈川県茅ヶ崎市*
	坂田山附の家／神奈川県大磯町*
	今宿の家／神奈川県横浜市*
1980	散田の共同住宅／東京都八王子市*
1981	祖師谷の家／東京都世田谷区*
1984	Project KO／東京都世田谷区*
1985	Project KA - 軽井沢厚生寮設計競技応募佳作案／長野県軽井沢町
	Project Z - 全労済会館設計競技応募入選案／東京都渋谷区
	Project CV - ヴェネツィア・ビエンナーレ参加案／イタリア
1986	Project SH - 湘南台文化センター設計競技応募佳作案／神奈川県藤沢市
	Project NT - 第二国立劇場設計競技応募案／東京都渋谷区
	Project S／神奈川県鎌倉市*
1987	Project UC／東京都新宿区
1988	House F／東京都品川区*
	Project M1, M2 - 宮の坂界隅設計競技応募案／東京都世田谷区
1989	Project TF - 東京国際フォーラム設計競技応募案／東京都千代田区
1990	Project MJ - パリ日仏文化会館設計競技応募案／フランス
1991	Project NAN - 新美南吉記念館設計競技応募案／愛知県半田市
	Project NAS - 那須野が原ハーモニーホール設計競技応募案／栃木県西那須野町
	Project NAR - 奈良県市民ホール国際建築設計競技応募案／奈良県奈良市
1992	コモンシティ星田／大阪府交野市［星田アーバンリビング設計競技最優秀作案（1988）］*
1993	新潟市民文化会館設計競技応募案／新潟県新潟市
1994	熊本市営託麻団地／熊本県熊本市*
	横浜国際客船ターミナル設計競技応募案／神奈川県横浜市
	千葉ライフ・パッサージュ千葉生涯学習センター設計競技応募案／千葉県千葉市
	東北歴史博物館設計競技応募案／宮城県多賀城市
	小町の舎設計競技応募案／京都府京丹後市
	東北近代文学館設計競技応募案／青森県青森市
1995	せんだい メディアテーク設計競技応募案／宮城県仙台市
	幕張ベイタウン・パティオス4番街／千葉県美浜区*
	長野市今井ニュータウン設計競技応募案／長野県長野市
	森山町立体育館設計競技応募案／長崎県北高木郡
1996	霧島彫刻ふれあいの森アートホール設計競技応募案／鹿児島県霧島市
	国立国会図書館関西館設計競技応募案／京都府相楽郡
	平田町タウンセンター設計競技応募案／山形県飽海郡
1997	函館公立大学プロポーザル案／北海道函館市
	宮城県立保健医療福祉中核施設全体施設設計競技応募案／宮城県

Catalogue of works

1969	House in Sanda, Hachioji, Tokyo*
1970	Townhouse in Minase, Hachioji, Tokyo*
1971	House in Nobuto, Chiba, Chiba Prefecture
1973	Kumono-Nagareyama House, Nagareyama, Chiba Prefecture*
	Project K, Chigasaki, Kanagawa Prefecture
1974	Project A, Yokohama, Kanagawa Prefecture
	Project N, Suwa, Nagano Prefecture
	Project S, Setagaya, Tokyo
1976	Townhouse in Daita, Setagaya, Tokyo*
1978	House in Nago, Chigasaki, Kanagawa Prefecture*
	House in Sakatayamatsuke, Oiso, Kanagawa Prefecture*
	House in Imajuku, Yokohama, Kanagawa Prefecture*
1980	Apartment House in Sanda, Hachioji, Tokyo*
1981	House in Soshigaya, Setagaya, Tokyo*
1984	Project KO, Setagaya, Tokyo*
1985	Project KA, Dormitory for Recreation, Karuizawa, Nagano Prefecture; competition, honourable mention
	Project Z, Zenrosai-Kaikan, Shibuya, Tokyo; competition, awarded
	Project CV, Venice Biennale, Venice, Italy
1986	Project SH, Shonandai Culture Centre, Fujisawa, Kanagawa Prefecture; competition, honourable mention
	Project NT, Second National Theatre, Shibuya, Tokyo; competition project
	Project S, Kamakura, Kanagawa Prefecture*
1987	Project UC, Shinjuku, Tokyo
1988	House F, Shinagawa, Tokyo*
	Project M1, M2, Development of Miyanosaka Area, Setagaya, Tokyo; competition
1989	Project TF, Tokyo International Forum, Chiyoda, Tokyo; competition
1990	Project MJ, La maison de la culture du Japon, Paris, France; competition
1991	Project NAN, Niimi Nankichi Memorial Museum, Handa, Aichi Prefecture; competition
	Project NAS, Nasunogahara Harmony Hall, Nishinasuno, Tochigi Prefecture; competition
	Project NAR, Nara Convention Hall, Nara, Nara Prefecture; competition
1992	Common City Hoshida, Katano, Osaka Prefecture [competition, first prize, 1988]*
1993	Niigata Civic Cultural Hall, Niigata, Niigata Prefecture; competition
1994	Kumamoto Takuma Housing, Kumamoto, Kumamoto Prefecture*
	Yokohama International Port Terminal, Yokohama, Kanagawa Prefecture; competition
	Chiba Life Passage Lifelong Education Centre, Chiba, Chiba Prefecture; competition
	Tohoku Historical Museum, Tagajo, Miyagi Prefecture; competition
	Komachi Museum, Kyotango, Kyoto Prefecture; competition
	Tohoku Modern Literature Museum, Aomori, Aomori Prefecture; competition
1995	Sendai Mediatheque, Sendai, Miyagi Prefecture; competition
	Housing in Makuhari Baytown, Mihami-ku, Chiba Prefecture*
	Imai New Town, Nagano, Nagano Prefecture; competition
	Moriyama Public Gymnasium, Kitatakagigun, Nagasaki Prefecture; competition
1996	Kirishima Art Hall, Airagun, Kagoshima Prefecture; competition
	National Diet Library Kansai Annex, Sourakugun, Kyoto Prefecture; competition
	Hirata Town Centre, Akumigun, Yamagata Prefecture; competition
1997	Hakodate University, Hakodate, Hokkaido Prefecture; competition
	Masterplan for Miyagi Prefectural Health and Welfare Centre, Miyagi Prefecture; competition

	ブエノスアイレス コンスタンティーニ美術館設計競技応募案／アルゼンチン
	KG. Mabohai Commercial Development Project／ブルネイ
1998	青森県立総合芸術公園設計競技応募案／青森県青森市
1999	House SA／神奈川県川崎市*
	新青森県立運動公園総合体育館設計競技応募案／青森県青森市
	青森県立美術館設計競技応募案／青森県青森市
	KG. Madang Shopping Complex Project／ブルネイ
2000	群馬県中里村新庁舎設計競技応募佳作案／群馬県中里村
	シンガポール経営大学プロポーザル佳作案／シンガポール
	佐世保港 近海航路旅客ターミナル設計競技応募案／長崎県佐世保市
2001	Hut T／山梨県山中湖村*
	松之山ステージ 自然科学館「森の学校」設計競技応募案／新潟県松之山
	南飛騨国際健康保養地健康学習センター設計競技応募案／岐阜県南飛騨
	青森市北国型集合住宅設計競技応募案／青森県青森市
2002	東村立新富弘美術館設計競技応募案／群馬県勢多郡
	新潟駅 駅舎・駅前広場計画提案競技応募案／新潟県新潟市
	勝山市健康福祉センター設計競技応募3等案／福井県勝山市
	Project M－東京工業大学緑が丘地区再編プロジェクト／東京都目黒区
	Project UM－東京工業大学ユニバーシティミュージアムプロジェクト／東京都目黒区
2003	南堀江 COCUE／大阪府大阪市
	Project KY1／東京都渋谷区
	Project KY2／東京都渋谷区
	Project KB／東京都渋谷区
	安中環境アートフォーラム設計競技応募案／群馬県安中市
	南方熊楠研究所設計競技応募案／和歌山県田辺市
	地球デザインスクール・セミナーハウス設計プロポーザル応募案／京都府宮津市
2004	Egota House A／東京都中野区［江古田の都市型集合住宅設計競技応募1等案（2002）］*
	熊野古道センター設計競技応募案／三重県尾鷲市
	松ヶ丘の集合住宅設計競技応募案／東京都中野区
2005	QUICO 神宮前／東京都渋谷区*
	岩見沢駅舎設計競技応募案／北海道岩見沢市
	立川市新庁舎設計競技応募案／東京都立川市
	南千束の集合住宅設計競技応募案／東京都大田区
	小田原市城下町ホール設計競技応募案／神奈川県小田原市
2006	工作連盟ジードルング・ヴィーゼンフェルト、ミュンヘン設計競技1等案／ドイツ*
	塩尻市市民交流センター設計競技応募案／長野県塩尻市
	ウィーン集合住宅設計競技応募案／オーストリア
2007	Cheltenham Art Gallery & Museum 設計競技応募案／イギリス
	小布施町図書館設計競技応募案／長野県小布施町
2008	水無瀬の別棟／東京都八王子市*
	浅草観光文化センター設計案コンペティション応募案／東京都台東区
	墨田区北斎館基本設計プロポーザル応募案／東京都墨田区
2009	東工大蔵前会館／東京都目黒区*
	群馬県農業技術センター設計競技応募案／群馬県伊勢崎市
	柏崎市新市民会館プロポーザル応募案／新潟県柏崎市
2010	ミュンヘン冬季オリンピック選手村設計競技入選案／ドイツ*
	共愛学園前橋国際大学4号館設計プロポーザル優秀賞案／群馬県前橋市
2011	宇土市立網津小学校／熊本県宇土市［宇土市立網津小学校設計プロポーザル1等案（2008）］*

	Constantini Museum, Buenos Aires, Argentina; competition
	KG. Mabohai Commercial Development Project, Brunei
1998	Prefectural Art Park, Aomori, Aomori Prefecture; competition
1999	House SA, Kawasaki, Kanagawa Prefecture*
	Prefectural Gymnastic Hall, Aomori, Aomori Prefecture; competition
	Prefectural Museum, Aomori, Aomori Prefecture; competition
	KG. Madang Shopping Complex Project, Brunei
2000	City Hall, Nakasato-mura, Gunma Prefecture; competition, honourable mention
	Singapore Management University, Singapore; competition, honourable mention
	Sasebo Ferry Terminal, Sasebo, Nagasaki Prefecture; competition
2001	Hut T, Yamanakako-mura, Yamanashi Prefecture*
	Matsunoyama Natural Science Museum, Matsunoyama, Niigata Prefecture; competition
	International Health Center, Minami-Hida, Gifu Prefecture; competition
	Northern Style Housing Complex, Aomori, Aomori Prefecture; competition
2002	New Tomihoro Museum, Setagun, Gunma Prefecture; competition
	Niigata Station, Niigata, Niigata Prefecture; competition
	Welfare Centre, Katsuyama, Fukui Prefecture; competition, third prize
	Project M, Tokyo Tech Midorigaoka Project, Meguro, Tokyo
	Project UM, Tokyo Tech University Museum Project, Meguro, Tokyo
2003	Minamihorie COCUE, Minamihorie, Osaka Prefecture
	Project KY1, Shibuya, Tokyo
	Project KY2, Shibuya, Tokyo
	Project KB, Shibuya, Tokyo
	Annaka Art Forum, Annaka, Gunma Prefecture; competition
	Minakata-Kumakusu Research Center, Tanabe, Wakayama Prefecture; competition
	Seminar House for Earth Design School, Miyazu, Kyoto Prefecture; competition
2004	Egota House A, Nakano, Tokyo [competition, first prize, 2002]*
	Kumano Kodo Centre, Owase, Mie Prefecture; competition
	Housing Complex in Matsugaoka, Nakano, Tokyo; competition
2005	QUICO Jingumae, Shibuya, Tokyo*
	Iwamizawa Station, Iwamizawa, Hokkaido Prefecture; competition
	City Hall, Tachikawa, Tokyo; competition
	Housing Complex in Minamisenzoku, Ota, Tokyo; competition
	Odawara Castle, Town Hall, Odawara, Kanagawa Prefecture; competition
2006	Werkbundsiedlung Wiesenfeld, Munich, Germany; competition, first prize
	Shiojiri City Community Center, Shiojiri, Nagano Prefecture; competition
	Collective Housing, Vienna, Austria; competition
2007	Cheltenham Art Gallery & Museum, Cheltenham, Great Britain; competition
	Obuse Library, Obuse, Nagano Prefecture; competition
2008	Minase Annex, Hachioji, Tokyo*
	Asakusa Culture Tourist Centre, Taito, Tokyo; competition
	Sumida Hokusai Museum, Sumida, Tokyo; competition
2009	Tokyo Tech Front, Meguro, Tokyo*
	Gunma Agriculture Centre, Isesaki, Gunma Prefecture; competition
	Municipal Hall, Kashiwazaki, Niigata Prefecture; competition
2010	Munich 2018 Winter Olympic Village, Germany; competition project, awarded*
	Maebashi Kyoai Gakuen College, Maebashi, Gunma Prefecture; competition, awarded
2011	Amitsu Primary School, Uto, Kumamoto Prefecture [competition, first prize, 2008]*

	ミュンヘン市地区計画コンペティション応募案／ドイツ
	熊本県立球磨工業高校管理棟改築設計競技応募案／熊本県人吉市
	遠山保育園改築プロポーザル応募案／宮城県宮城郡七ヶ浜町
	上州富岡駅プロポーザル応募案／群馬県富岡市
2012	岐南町新庁舎等設計者選定設計競技佳作案／岐阜県岐南町
	釜石市災害復興公営住宅プロポーザル応募案／岩手県釜石市
	七ヶ浜中学校建設基本・実地設計プロポーザル応募案／宮城県七ヶ浜町
	富岡市新庁舎建設設計プロポーザル応募案／群馬県富岡市
2013	広島県立呉南特別支援学校プロポーザル最優秀案／広島県呉市
	改築 散田の家／東京都八王子市*
	Egota House B／東京都中野区 [江古田の都市型集合住宅設計競技応募1等案 (2002)]*
2014	佐賀県歯科医師会館プロポーザル最優秀賞／佐賀県佐賀市
	常州工学院国際学術交流センター計画／中国常州市
	寧波東銭湖会所計画／中国寧波市
	上海当代芸術博物館計画／中国上海市
2015	府中市新庁舎プロポーザル応募案／東京都府中市
	Project AO／神奈川県川崎市

* 講演で紹介される作品

	Urban Design Plan, Munich, Germany; competition
	Kuma Technical High School, Hitoyoshi, Kumamoto Prefecture; competition
	Toyama Nursery School, Shichigahama, Miyagi Prefecture; competition
	Joshu-Tomioka Station, Tomioka, Gunma Prefecture; competition
2012	City Hall, Ginan, Gifu Prefecture; competition, honourable mention
	Kamaishi Reconstruction Housing Project, Kamaishi, Iwate Prefecture; competition
	Shichigahama Junior High School, Shichigahama, Miyagi Prefecture; competition
	City Hall, Tomioka, Gunma Prefecture; competition
2013	Kure South Special Needs School, Kure, Hiroshima Prefecture; competition, first prize
	Renovation House in Sanda, Hachioji, Tokyo*
2014	Egota House B, Nakano, Tokyo [competition, first prize, 2002]*
	Saga Dental Association Building, Saga, Saga Prefecture; competition, first prize
	Changzhou Institute of Technology International Exchange Centre Project, Changzhou, China
	Ningbo Dongqian Lake Clubhouse Project, Ningbo, China
	Shanghai Power Station of Art Project, Shanghai, China
2015	City Hall, Fuchu, Tokyo; competition
	Project AO, Kawasaki, Kanagawa Prefecture

* Buildings and projects presented in the lecture

ベアロッハー太央

1985年京都生まれ。スイス連邦工科大学チューリッヒ校で建築を学ぶ。2011年同大学卒業。その後メンドリジオ建築アカデミーでアシスタントを務める。2014年より自身の設計活動をチューリッヒではじめる。

サミュエル・スカッサビア

1984年イタリア、マントヴァ生まれ。ミラノ工科大学とメンドリジオ建築アカデミーで建築を学ぶ。2011年メンドリジオ建築アカデミーにて学位取得。ミラノ工科大学、メンドリジオ建築アカデミー、およびスイス連邦工科大学チューリッヒ校でアシスタントを務める。2014年より自身の設計活動をチューリッヒではじめる。

長谷川豪

1977年埼玉県生まれ。2002年東京工業大学大学院修士課程修了。2002−04年西沢大良建築設計事務所勤務を経て、2005年長谷川豪建築設計事務所設立。2009−11年東京工業大学ほか非常勤講師、2012−14年メンドリジオ建築アカデミー客員教授、2014年オスロ建築大学客員教授を歴任。2015年東京工業大学大学院博士課程修了。工学博士。

Tao Baerlocher

Born in 1985 in Kyoto, Japan. He studied Architecture at the ETH Zurich (Diploma 2011). He worked as a teaching assistant at the Accademia di Architettura di Mendrisio. Since 2014 he has worked as an independent architect in Zurich.

Samuele Squassabia

Born in 1984 in Mantua, Italy. He studied Architecture at the Politecnico di Milano and the Accademia di Architettura di Mendrisio (Diploma 2011). He worked as a teaching assistant at the Accademia di Architettura di Mendriso, the ETH Zurich and the Politecnico di Milano. Since 2014 he has worked as an independent architect in Zurich.

Go Hasegawa

Born in 1977 in Saitama, Japan. He completed the master course at the Graduate School of Science and Engineering, Tokyo Institute of Technology in 2002. He worked at Taira Nishizawa Architects and established Go Hasegawa & Associates in 2005. Between 2009–2011 he taught as a Visiting Lecturer at the Tokyo Institute of Technology and other universities in Japan. He was Visiting Professor at the Accademia di Architettura di Mendrisio between 2012–2014 and the Oslo School of Architecture and Design in 2014. In 2015 he completed his doctorate at the Tokyo Institute of Technology.

坂本一成・講演

著者：坂本一成
編集／企画：ベアロッハー太央、サミュエル・スカッサビア
出版プロジェクト：Quart出版社、リーヌス・ウィルツ
まえがき：ベアロッハー太央、サミュエル・スカッサビア
あとがき：長谷川豪
英語翻訳：ベアロッハー太央
英語校閲：ベンヤミン・リーベルト
レイアウト：ベアロッハー太央、サミュエル・スカッサビア／Quart出版社、リーヌス・ウィルツ
製版：Printeria, Luzern
印刷：DZA Druckerei zu Altenburg GmbH

© Copyright 2015
Quart出版社、ハインツ・ウィルツ
無断で本書の全体または一部の複写・複製を禁じます。
ISBN 978-3-03761-106-7

本書は独語＋日本語版でも出版されています。(ISBN 978-3-03761-105-0)

Quart Publishers
Denkmalstrasse 2, CH-6006 Luzern
www.quart.ch

写真
新建築社：p.18, 22-23, 26, 27, 28, 31, 42, 43, 44, 46, 48, 50, 52, 54, 56, 58, 59, 60-61, 62, 78, 106, 120, 123
[p.22-23, 26, 28, 31 (画像提供：DAAS)]
新倉孝雄：p.20, 21
藤塚光政：p.24, 104, 107
田中宏明：p.30
多木浩二：p.34, 36-37, 38
アトリエ・アンド・アイ 坂本一成研究室：p.40, 41, 57, 66, 68, 70, 80, 81, 82, 86, 87, 88, 89, 90, 91, 92, 96, 98, 100, 102-103, 108, 110, 112-113, 114, 118, 119, 124, 126, 128-129, 132, 136, 138, 139, 140, 142, 144-145, 146, 147, 148, 149, 152, 154, 155, 156, 158, 159, 160-161
大橋富夫：p.72-73, 74, 84-85
ホンマタカシ：p.101
畑拓（彰国社）：p.122
樋口貴彦：p.168

Kazunari Sakamoto. Lecture

Author: Kazunari Sakamoto, Tokyo
Editor/Concept: Tao Baerlocher, Zurich and Samuele Squassabia, Zurich
Publication project: Quart Publishers, Linus Wirz
Foreword: Tao Baerlocher and Samuele Squassabia
Afterword: Go Hasegawa, Tokyo
Translation Japanese-English: Tao Baerlocher
Text editing English: Benjamin Liebelt, Berlin
Graphic Design: Tao Baerlocher and Samuele Squassabia; Quart Publishers, Linus Wirz
Lithos: Printeria, Luzern
Printing and binding: DZA Druckerei zu Altenburg GmbH

© Copyright 2015
Quart Publishers Lucerne, Heinz Wirz
All rights reserved
ISBN 978-3-03761-106-7

This book is also published in Japanese-German (ISBN 978-3-03761-105-0)

Quart Publishers
Denkmalstrasse 2, CH-6006 Luzern
www.quart.ch

Photos:
Shinkenchiku-sha, Tokyo: p. 18, 22–23, 26, 27, 28, 31, 42, 43, 44, 46, 48, 50, 52, 54, 56, 58, 59, 60–61, 62, 78, 106, 120, 123 [p. 22–23, 26, 28, 31 (Photo by DAAS)]
Niikura Takao, Tokyo: p. 20, 21
Fujitsuka Mitsumasa, Tokyo: p. 24, 104, 107
Hiroaki Tanaka, Tokyo: p. 30
Koji Taki, Tokyo: p. 34, 36–37, 38
Atelier and I, Kazunari Sakamoto Architectural Laboratory, Tokyo: p. 40, 41, 57, 66, 68, 70, 80, 81, 82, 86, 87, 88, 89, 90, 91, 92, 96, 98, 100, 102–103, 108, 110, 112–113, 114, 118, 119, 124, 126, 128–129, 132, 136, 138, 139, 140, 142, 144–145, 146, 147, 148, 149, 152, 154, 155, 156, 158, 159, 160–161
Tomio Ohashi, Tokyo: p. 72–73, 74, 84–85
Takashi Homma, Tokyo: p. 101
Taku Hata (Shokokusha Photographers), Tokyo: p. 122
Takahiko Higuchi, Iida: p. 168